SMILE, LAUGH, AND BE HAPPY

The Culture of God's Kingdom is
The King's Will For You

Apostle Dr. Bacer J. Baker

Dominion Unlimited Publications

Copyright © 2022 Apostle, Dr. Bacer J. Baker

Smile, Laugh and Be Happy – The Culture of God's Kingdom is The King's Will For You by Apostle, Dr. Bacer J. Baker
Copyright © 2011- 2022 by Apostle, Dr. Bacer J. Baker
Original "Happy Songs" – Copyright © 2011-2022 by Lonzine L. Lee
Cover Design: David Munoz Prophetic Art

Print ISBN: 979-8-9859944-3-8
eBook ISBN: 979-8-9859944-7-6
Printed in the United States of America.
All rights reserved solely by the author. The views expressed in this book are not necessarily those of the publisher. The author guarantees all contents of this book are original and do not infringe upon any laws or legal rights of any other person or work, and that this book is not libelous, plagiarized or in any other way illegal. No part of this book may be reproduced in any form without the permission of the author. Short extracts may be used for review purposes.
Unless otherwise indicated, Bible quotations are taken from The New King James Version. Copyright © 1982 by Thomas Nelson.
Scriptures marked KJV are from the King James Version of the Bible.
Scripture quotations marked (AMPC) are taken from the Amplified Bible, Copyright © 1954, 1958, 1962, 1964, 1965, 1987 by The Lockman Foundation. Used by permission. www.lockman.org.
Scripture quotations marked CEV are from the Contemporary English Version Copyright © 1991, 1992, 1995 by American Bible Society, Used by Permission.
Scriptures marked ESV are from The Holy Bible, English Standard Version® (ESV®), copyright © 2001 by Crossway, a publishing ministry of Good News Publishers. Used by permission. All rights reserved.
Scripture quotations marked (NIV) are taken from the Holy Bible, New International Version®, NIV®. Copyright © 1973, 1978, 1984 by Biblica, Inc.™ Used by permission of Zondervan. All rights reserved worldwide. www.zondervan.com.
Scripture taken from THE MIRROR. Copyright © 2012. By Francois du Toit. Used by permission of The Author. All rights reserved.
Scriptures marked TMB are Scripture taken from The Message. Copyright © 1993, 1994, 1995, 1996, 2000, 2001, 2002. Used by permission of NavPress Publishing Group.
Scriptures marked VOICE are taken from The Voice™. Copyright © 2012 by Ecclesia Bible Society. Used by permission. All rights reserved.

CONTENTS

Title Page	
Copyright	
Foreword	
Acknowledgments	1
Endorsements	2
An Apostolic Introduction to joying	5
A Biblical Perspective on Happiness	9
The Principle of Joying	11
The Master Key	15
Signature Key	19
Happy Key #1	27
Happy Key #2	41
Happy Key #3	51
Happy Key #4	59
Happy Key #5	65
Why We Can Sing Happy Songs…	70
The Joy of The Lord is Triumphant Over Grief	73
Happy Key #6	87
Happy Key #7	99
Happy Key #8	105
Happy Key #9	113

THE PRAISE FOR YOUR GOODNESS SONG	127
MY HAPPY DANCE & CLAP SONG	140
SMILE. LAUGH. BE HAPPY.	143
FINAL WORDS	155
Bibliography	158
Books By This Author	161

One Smile. That's all it takes! The atmosphere will respond to an obedient smile.

Smiling is a KEY. The world is waiting for you to down and smile!

- David Munoz
David Munoz Prophetic Art

FOREWORD

Societal anxiety and current circumstances have fostered ever-increasing conditions of a hopelessness that pervades people's consciousness on an almost subliminal level. We gasp and weep over the degradation that we see so blatantly and ask, much like the listeners of Peters' impassioned discourse which resulted in the question "What must we do to be saved"?

Salvation for several centuries has been diminished to a simple, ritualistic formula that severely underestimates and leaves supposed "believers" sensing that something is still missing… but what? We said the prayer, we confessed our sins and got up feeling good, but no real transformation seems to have been enacted. We act on our "decision" of that time with degrees of devotion, yet inwardly we know that the conscious still feels somewhat bleak.

Over time our devotion de-escalates to redundancy for the sake of appearance, and we move into a state of wishful thinking in whisper hopes of making it to heaven. Sadly, this is the reality of an ever-growing number of those in the modern-day church. Our faith is more active in listening to the 24-hour cable news network and sharing in their opinions instead of knowing the Superior Reality that Kingdom Culture was designed from the beginning to provide for us.

Joy was not "created." It IS the Culture of the Triune existence in their unity that was the atmosphere in which the visible expression of His Image and Likeness was brought forth. The RESULT of that joy was a happiness that was concluded in the Word of The Lord saying, *"It is Very Good"*!

Listen intently to the heavenly echo that resounded in a rapturous elation at the perfection of the design that even God Himself, uttering those words, declared that He could do no better. This was the apex of His immediate and permanent calculation! Humankind revealing His Image and Likeness to all that was brought into the visible realm for the provision of humankind, all the while humankind was created wholly and solely for God!

In the Life of our Authentic Design, humankind was to share in this Joy as his allotted portion, yet fear was introduced into his soul by deception of the one of the fallen mind. Humankind accepted that in the perception of the false image, he was in lack and God had withheld something from him.

The awareness of the cultural atmosphere of Heaven, which was revealed in the visible realm as light, began to diminish. Darkness swept over his soul. The absence of Light always speaks of chaos as the absence of darkness speaks of Order. Light always reveals structure and gives recognition and reality in mankind's ability to perceive as his Creator does. In humankind sharing in the Trinity's Perfect Culture, Joy gave clarity to man's vision which brought order to all of creation, man was designed to have dominion over.

Sorrow became the result of man's judgement in choosing outside of his allotment. *"In sorrow you will bear children, and in sorrow you will cultivate the earth from where you came."* Sorrow was the bread, or that which fed the fallen mind, that eventually prevailed in man's consciousness until the very remembrance of their Original Life was hidden in darkness.

Suddenly, in a time of great depression, sadness, and sorrow, a Word pierces through the blackened obscurity of mankind's soul offering to us, once again, a restored Salient Cognizance which resonated deep within man's consciousness. Although placed there by the Progenitor Himself, it laid dormant, hidden behind a veil and unrecognizable by the shamed and degenerate soul, yet the sharp edge The Word, divided the spirit and soul of man and revealed the thoughts and intents of God's very Heart.

The Birth of Messiah would Herald the Salvation and Restoration of mankind. The Incarnation of Messiah, taking on the form of man, would sufficiently herald the Grand Announcement and set man free from the slavery of soul. Shepherding man from his Identity Gone Astray back into the Enlightened Atmosphere of Joy. The Culture of the Heavenly Realm, which was always to be the Fathers Home, our place of security, provision, companionship, and full acceptance. Joy Realized.

> *The people walking in darkness see a bright light; light shines on those who live in a land of deep darkness. 3 You have enlarged the nation; you give them great joy. They rejoice in your presence as harvesters rejoice; as warriors celebrate when they divide up the plunder. Isaiah 9:2-3 NET*

This is prophesied to be a Gleaming Luminosity that would conquer the darkness of sorrow and be the Gift of Righteousness that was to Redeem, Reclaim, and Redistribute the Inheritance of Kingdom Culture back to its Origins in the Visible Realm. Joy Unspeakable, creating a fully recognizable Glory that brought Clarity to the Nations made up of all humankind that was blown away and became chaff, was NOW declared the Harvest

and the Great Spoil of the Overcoming One! JOY prevailed and HAPPINESS became LOVE'S Expression in the
superior Reality of the NOW Covenant.

Too often, by way of underestimation and sheer ignorance, religion attempts to sway us back into the place of light absence and persuades us to again become active in the poneras system. Poneras is the koine Greek word used for the word translated "evil" in the Septuagint. The Old Testament, written by 72 Jewish scholars in Greek and completed in 132 B.C. The word *poneras* is defined as a system of Hardship, Toil and Labor by Dr. Thayer. That which produces sorrow.

This is and has always been the fruit of the tree of Good and Evil. The I-Am-Not tree, coined by Francois Du Toit, defines our existence in the absence of Joy. The endgame of this tree. Our own judgement apart from Progenitors Faith which results are always the same, Failure, Shame, and the sense of Separation.

In Nehemiah 8, we see how Israel had returned from the first Diaspora from Babylon after 70 years of exile from their homeland, to rebuild the Wall and the Temple and begin the daunting Process of Restoration. Those who had a heart to do the work were allowed to make the pilgrimage home while facing multiple challenges. At a certain time, Ezra, Nehemiah, and the returning Levites found a copy of the Torah. They called a Sacred Assembly to Order, and Ezra spent six to seven hours reading from Torah to a company of people that most had never even heard the Word read aloud from the actual writings.

As was a product of the grieved and darkened soul, shame swept over them and they began to weep, so much so that the Leadership Assembly (representative
of the Ascension Gift Ministries of the NOW Day) stood up and spoke aloud. In Verse 9 they declared boldly, *"This day is Sacred to the Eternal! It is not a day for mourning and weeping!"* In verse 10

they encouraged them to return to their homes and prepare for a time JOY and Feasting welcoming all to their tables no matter what their individual status! Grief and Shame over their history was disallowed and it was declared *"Let the Eternals Joy be your protection!"*

This Prophetic Pointer is concluded in Christ in the NOW Dimension! Grace and Truth have come to us, all humankind, by way of The Incarnation to Co-Include us in the work declared by Messiah as Finished! God In Christ leveling man up into the Authentic Life of His Design, Operationally Functional in Spiritual Spatial Awareness in the Immediacy of the Presence of Immanuel.

ABBA Yahweh ever living In Us, Among Us and Through US! Joy and Happiness are NOW the Present Reality of The Eternalness of ABBA being Our Life! His Faith from the beginning NOW known in the Shared Life of the Culture of the Kingdom...The Atmosphere of JOY!
Listen intently, hear accurately, and learn experientially from Apostle Baker's years of applicable wisdom to find your heart soaring with fresh revelation for Spiritual Security in the Atmosphere of Heaven...

Apostle Robin Beach
Kingdom Leader, Teacher and Author
Host: *A Journey to Discovery*
Prairie Grove, Arkansas, USA

ACKNOWLEDGMENTS

This is the revised, expanded edition of the original book I wrote, published, and recorded on CD in 2011.

I continue to thank my Father God for my salvation through Jesus Christ, and Holy Spirit for Your inspiration in writing this book. *Thank You for trusting me to write about Your desire for us to be and have happy thoughts.*

I would like to acknowledge and thank the following people for their contributions to this project:

Lonzine Lee: *Thanks, daughter for writing the songs that accompany the book.*

David Munoz, to think that you designed the picture of joy cover art in the same year that God told me to write the original version of this book. Look at God!*Thank you for sharing your art with us all.*

To the ministry staff, church members and friends of Astounding Love: *Thank you for your prayers and enthusiasm in support of this project.*

ENDORSEMENTS

You'll never be sad another day in your life!

Smile, Laugh, and Be Happy is loaded with simple, life transforming principles that will have you smiling, singing, and laughing by the end of each chapter. The believer should be overflowing with the joy of the Lord, and abounding in the peace of Christ, yet so many are depressed, distressed, and miserable.

I believe that this simple little book is destined to break the yoke of depression, and is sure to be God's remedy for the emotional ills of the church.

Dr. Mark T. Jones Sr.
Manifestations Worldwide Inc.
Tampa, Florida
"I live for the manifestation of the sons of God."

Apostle Baker's laughter is contagious to say the least. What amazes me the most is her joy and peace has lasted throughout the forty-plus years of my association with her life and ministry. Smile, Laugh, and Be Happy is an accurate presentation of God's total intentions for His people to live by here on earth. It reveals and completely exposes the force of the joy of the Lord to the Believers. The quality of this book is written from the quality of a life well-lived.

Each chapter draws you in deeper and deeper in the flow of

Kingdom living here on earth. Verse by verse, Apostle Baker reveals the foundation for every truth that is revealed and established in her writings. Many today have not found true joy and laughter in their salvation experience. The Bible says, *"the Joy of the Lord is your strength."* Apostle Baker points the reader to the Word of God. Nothing is written or inferred that is not a witness of the canon of Scripture.

Apostle Baker is a close friend and confidante. Our time together in ministry has brought forth much fruit in the advancement of the Kingdom of God. She is a woman of God and a Son. A woman of prayer and an intercessor. She is a woman of great compassion and grace. She operates as a repairer of the breach and a restorer of old waste places. But the most important thing to me is that she is my Sister!

Big Love (Ap. Calvin Cook)
Apostle and Founder of Golden Altar Ministries
World Outreach Church
San Jose, California
Member of the Love & Unity Senior Council

One of my greatest joys and honor is to be both the biological/spiritual daughter, and the spiritual son of Apostle Bacer J. Baker. She birthed me into the earth on an August day, birthed me into Christ on a day in January, and then as God healed the fractured parts of our relationship, I became her spiritual son in the faith. Why a son when I am a woman? Because of Jesus.

Through my mom the apostle (and her fellow ministers), I learned and continue to learn more of the mysteries of this so great salvation and the Kingdom of God. But here's what I want to share.

I had the honor to again edit and get this book prepared for you, beloved readers. And my, my, my how it ministered joy, peace, grace, happiness, healing, and breakthrough to my soul. Even as I typed, God worked in me for His greater glory. And He will do the same for you.

It is my prayer that you enjoy the experience the Lord has in store for you as you journey through this book. Have fun. Take it as God's message to you. Sing the songs. Do the exercises. Most of all, I encourage you to do what the Laughing Doctor says. *Smile, Laugh, and Be Happy!* Because joy truly is the culture of God's Kingdom, and **it is the King's will for you**. Blessings and much astounding love to you.

Lonzine Lee, MBA
Pastor/Teacher, Astounding Love!
A Global Church Fellowship & Training Center
Principal, Dominion Unlimited Publications
Manteca, CA USA

AN APOSTOLIC INTRODUCTION TO JOYING

Please understand that God, our Father does not want us sad. This book is HIS idea, not mine. He said to write a Happy Book because, *"...too many of MY people are sad."*

Numerous changes occur in our lives as we learn to walk in the Spirit of the Fear of the Lord. For me, the most significant changes that I have experienced since the original edition of this book was released have come from an immersion into the message of the Kingdom of God and the Spirit of the Fear of the Lord. By gaining a clearer understanding of the message of the Kingdom of God. I've begun to fear Him in a completely different way.

The desire to return to my early days of Creation Therapy (learning, teaching, and ministering about the five temperaments (choleric, melancholy, phlegmatic, sanguine, and supine) that God has placed in us has increased. In secular psychology, man focuses on four temperaments. But God entrusted us with five temperaments (no one person has them all), and He has stirred up my inward desire to go further in my understanding how uniquely different the temperament blends and layers are expressed through different individuals.

Creation Therapy or temperament counseling is a Biblically

based approach to human behavior based on five temperaments of God. "In the beginning God created the heavens and the earth… For You formed my inward parts; You covered me in my mother's womb. I will praise You, for I am fearfully and wonderfully made; Marvelous are Your works, And that my soul knows very well." (Genesis 1:1, Psalm 139:13-14)

In case you don't know, to understand the purpose of the temperaments that God used and has woven within us is not a fad or trending movement to be studied for a season. The temperaments of God are not a teaching or mere psychological methodology. We have been arrogant in our understanding of stewarding Kingdom treasures.

The temperaments are God's divine expressions of Himself released into the earth through His people. You cannot read about them or take an online test and walk away knowing everything you need to know about yourself. You see, God placed a combination of His own five temperaments inside each of us. In order to overcome every obstacle and manifest true Kingdom power in the pattern of Jesus Christ, He has made every expression of His strength, mercy, grace, power, and joy that we need available to us.

Answers to every situation can be found by learning the way that the Spirit of the Living God sees, hears, speaks, moves, and acts. He has woven Himself into us so that as He is, so are we in this world!

We know that everything in the world system is hostile to His kingdom but walking in Him makes a difference. As we walk with Him in daily fellowship, He walks us through hostile environments, and equips us with the ability to triumph in every situation with joy. Allow the joy of His Kingdom to spring up within and flow out of you. As Kingdom peace permeates your inner being, you will come into Heaven's understanding of what it means to smile, laugh, and be happy regardless of what tries to come against you. Just like Jesus did.

Because of God in us and us in Him, we are enabled and expected to allow His Kingdom joy to manifest His peace, faith, lovingkindness, and other divine attributes to operate in every aspect of our lives. For every situation that we face, God has provided a Kingdom solution. That's because we are the righteousness of God, kings and priests unto Himself. He is the King of kings, the King of kings within us.

As truly we walk, as we live, as we sit, as we think, as we lay in bed at night, whatever it is that we do, the spirit of this world without Him is still a hostile environment. Why? Because it wants to destroy the king ship within us, our ability to exercise our privilege to obey the King. And that obedience that we walk in is also an expression of our choice to trust Him alone.

Through every expression of His nature, the Lord is saying to His sons,

"This is what I think of you, I have placed Myself in this form in you, so that you can walk in this hostile environment, and still allow My joy to be in you. And then you can reply to hostility with smiling, being happy, allowing the happiness to spring out of the joy of Me to manifest rather than all of the complaining. You can speak of what was as if it never was. You can speak with a voice of joy."

Apostle Bacer J. Baker,
Ph.D. in Psychology
The Laughing Doctor
September 2022

A BIBLICAL PERSPECTIVE ON HAPPINESS

Happy is the man that findeth wisdom, and the man that getteth understanding. Proverbs 3:13

A TYPICAL AMERICAN DICTIONARY DEFINES *happy* as being cheery, content or satisfied. The Hebrew word *"esher"* is defined as *"happy* or *blessed."* According to the Bible, a happy person is someone that finds God's wisdom and gains understanding of God's word.

Why does the Bible say that the person that finds wisdom is happy? (Proverbs 3:13) Because this is a person who has learned that the payoff of attaining God's wisdom garners more profit than silver, gold or rubies. Wisdom is deemed incomparable to anything that a person might desire; offering long life, riches, honor, delight, and satisfaction. (Proverbs 8:11, 16:16)

According to God, happiness is for the people that choose Him. (Psalm 144:15)

Some believe that financial wealth provides happiness. Financial wealth apart from a relationship with Jesus Christ is poverty. Wealth does not guarantee happiness. It may seem as if financial wealth is worth having, regardless of the cost. But the truth of the matter is there are a lot of people who daily make themselves poor by the choice of pursuing money, thinking that they don't need God. To those without a relationship with God through Jesus Christ poverty will remain, for their wealth is not eternal.

Being happy is choosing to trust and see life God's way. Thereby in making this choice we are choosing a lifestyle of joy and happiness. At any given moment, regardless of what is happening all around us, we are choosing our outlook and the feelings and emotions we will have to conform to.

Even when people treat us unkindly, we can choose joy and be happy because *we make the choice to be happy*. No matter what you have thought or been told, *nothing or anyone outside of yourself can make you happy or sad*. Do not allow anyone to usurp your power to think good God-filled thoughts. Appoint no one but yourself to be the one to choose your personal happiness.

We are each responsible to acquire and maintain *our own* personal joy. No one else gets that privilege. Remember, God wants you to think and be content, but *you have to agree and act upon it*.

THE PRINCIPLE OF JOYING

ELEVEN YEARS AGO, I WAS minding my own business while thinking about some of the unhappy people I was counseling in therapy. I was thinking about how those who identified with being called Christians and Believers were operating from a purely human mindset.

The things they allowed themselves to believe about God and themselves kept them from true joy and happiness. That's when I heard God say to me, *"Write a Happy Book and put it on CD."*

Being in my vocation and profession for over 40 years, I have seen scores of people go up and down emotionally because of the circumstances or just the condition of their thought life. These traps have also snared me occasionally, and I know how defeating it can be. When God told me to do this book and CD project, I obeyed. Obedience is the first key to happiness. So I present you the revised, expanded version of my obedience to His command.

Smile, Laugh, and Be Happy is for anyone who wants to stop the madness of allowing feelings of sadness, depression, fear, and anxiety to change your moods from happy or joyful to sad and moody. The purpose of this powerful little book is for you to have a *"Run-to Quick* reference on 'What God says about my situation.'" Run to Him, and then do what He says.

This is a childlike faith book with a simple and seemingly silly approach, but it will create profound and permanent changes in your life if you decide, "I will run to what God says and thinks about my situation." Receive these tools as a personal gift designed by God Himself just for you. It really is.

Back when Bobby McFerrin told us, *"Don't worry, be happy,"* it was a catchy little song releasing Kingdom wisdom. Yet as relevant as Mr. McFerrin's message remains in modern times, the phrase, *"Don't worry"* did not originate with man. God said it first, and He says it often in His Word.

The message is simple and powerful. Let it be one of the easiest things for you, God's masterpiece, to embrace. Obey God's word, and to loosely reference a song title from Stevie Wonder, *"Don't you worry about a thing!"* That's what the Lord says to me.

"Don't you worry about a thing. Because when you worry, you magnify the wrong thoughts about ME."

God wants you to think about good things. Kingdom keys, exhortations, fun little original songs with familiar melodies, and a variety of what we call "happy facts, happy declarations, and joy keys" fill this book. These are things that you can so easily incorporate into your daily life. So let's be a smile to Him by using our God-given faith and win every challenge.

God has equipped us to restore broken relationships and lost dreams. We are here to help people who worry about the economy, sickness, diseases, and life's problems to change and start to have joyous thoughts. By spreading laughter we can show them how to turn around every situation.

Remember God created us to agree and work with Him, obeying and rising above the problems of life. God actually instructs us not to be anxious about anything, so let's obey. Let's give Him praise and expect His peace to guard and protect our hearts and minds from the toxins of anxiety, depression, and fear.

Here's a tool for your arsenal: *The Principle of Joying.*

Joying is one of my personal dictionary words. [Yes, I have my own dictionary.] Joying is defined, "to have a full-time attitude of joy in God," which includes being joy-filled no matter what's going on in the economy, the state of the world, your family, business, and everything else that pertains to life.

No matter what is going on, remember that your future is secure. Joying is a Kingdom of God tool that will be health, prosperity, and emotional well-being for you and defeat for Satan's kingdom. Always remember that you have a powerful, everlasting, unbreakable covenant with Almighty God. You got it when you became born from above.

The keys presented in this small book are given in response to the great many people in the earth that take the wrong things seriously. There is more to smile and laugh about then there is to cry about. We have many more reasons and things to rejoice about than we do to complain. Sometimes you just need a key to unlock the door that leads to the right way of thinking.

A merry heart, like a medicine, does your body good and releases power to perform from within. Everything that you need has already been provided for you through Yeshua HaMashiach, Jesus Christ. He said that *"It is finished."* And so it is.

Because He did it all, you don't have to worry. You can smile, you can laugh, you can be happy. He completed the work to provide everything you or I need in order to succeed in this life and the one to come. Jesus said that He has given you all things that pertain to life and godliness. It has already been done for you.

This means that all of the problems or circumstances that

you encounter in this life have already been taken care of. You can count it all joy, because it is already done. All we have to do is to follow the path that has been laid out for us. Jesus paid it all.

I encourage you to choose to live in the Kingdom of God, which is righteousness, peace and joy in the Holy Spirit. It is my prayer that as you embrace God's words in these pages, you allow these keys to release you into joy and remind you that you have something to smile about.

And once you start smiling, you'll begin to laugh and splinter the foundation of any unhappiness in your soul. Don't forget, you are to always rejoice in the Lord.
Happiness is option number one. Choose it!

Scriptures: Matthew 18:3, Matthew 6:25-32, Genesis 1:26-27, Philippians 4:6-10, Proverbs 17:22, John 19:20, 2Peter 1:3, Romans 14:17, Philippians 4:4

THE MASTER KEY

Obedience is Better

"...What is more pleasing to the Lord: your burnt offerings and sacrifices or your obedience to His voice? Listen! Obedience is better than sacrifice, and submission is better than offering the fat of rams." 1Samuel 15:22 NLT

THE IDEA OF OBEDIENCE TO GOD is almost archaic to those of a darkened understanding. Modern so-called enlightened or "woke" culture operates with a common mindset of rebellion and revolution against established truth, be it spiritual or historical. Yet the principle of obedience is the essential key to living in the joy and happiness that God has provided for you.

In the scripture referenced above, the Old Testament defines obedience as *"hearing intelligently"* and *"giving attention or an ear to."* It also means to *"show regard, listen, understand,* and *witness"* or attest to what the speaker or instructor is saying. Interestingly, the word does not describe a loss of freedom or an inability to function as an individual.

We have a God that loves us with eternal love. He has made wonderful plans for all of our lives, and it is His intent to give us hope and a future.

> *"I know what I'm doing. I have it all planned out — plans to take care of you, not abandon you, plans to give you the future you hope for." Jeremiah 29:11 TMB*

So why does He want us to obey Him? The short answer is so that He can do good things for us. Consider the beginning of the history of mankind. God instructed the man named Adam to refrain from eating from one tree in the Garden of Eden.

We don't know how many trees there were in Eden, but we do know that Adam and his wife had access to all of them any time of the day or night. Only one tree was not theirs to eat from. But they did eat from it, and in effect, they chose not to obey God's command.

Not the happiest day in their lives, I'm sure.

Before they ate, it was *very* well with them. They had no pressures and no heavy-duty responsibilities. In fact, God took care of all of their needs. However, they chose to listen to an interloper's words and disregarded God's instruction. After they ate from that one tree, things weren't as good.

With that one decision to disobey God, they lost dominion of the ground they once controlled. Evicted from their home, they had to learn how to work for food, and they were no longer recipients of the full goodness and fellowship that God had for them. I think they were not happy people, and there probably was not much joy either. Maybe that's why many are not happy now, because of choices to disobey God's protective orders.

When Jesus walked the earth, He lived a life of obedience.

He walked in the fullness of God's word, taking it upon Himself to fulfill every command. He resisted the temptations of the devil and walked in victorious power and authority throughout His life.

As you read through the Gospels (Matthew, Mark, Luke, and John) you see how Jesus joyed in talking to God, doing what God instructed, and sharing the goodness of the Father with all who came to Him for love, healing, deliverance, provision, peace, and fellowship. He was an exciting person to be around, a shining Light in a world that had seen nothing like Him before. He delighted in obeying God.

All of this anointing, power, authority, blessing and goodness came about because Jesus obeyed the Father's commands. He went where the Father told Him to go, doing good to and for others, driving out the oppression of the devil. He lived a life that blessed others.

All that proclaim Jesus as Lord can do likewise as we also spend each day choosing to obey the directives of God. We too will shine forth as lights in a world of darkness and draw people to God.

We will pleasingly be carriers of the goodness of God, vessels of His love, healing, deliverance, provision, peace, and fellowship pouring into the lives and homes of people around us..

This is so exciting!

It's something to rejoice about. God's will for each of us revolve around our cooperating with His plan. He will reveal different parts of the plan as we allow ourselves to be carried along in the flow and tide of obedience that He has made available to us.

We are dwelling places for the Living God. Obedience establishes the dominion or royal kingdom reign [*basileia* is the Greek translation] of the King of kings and the Lord of lords.

Just like Jesus, the power to establish the Kingdom of God here on earth is within us. We are on earth to let people know that wherever we are, surely the Kingdom of Heaven (and its royal blessings) is among them.

Obedience is better. We have no need for a Plan B. Obeying God is better than trying to do some type of penance to make up for our shortcomings. God forgives our failures when we come to Him. He forgives us of our sins, and He also equipped us to succeed by placing His own Spirit within us.

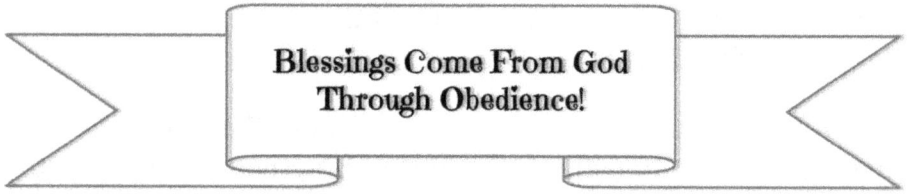

Blessings Come From God Through Obedience!

Obedience is the first key to true happiness. In fact, it is the Master key. As we walk with Him in the cool of the day and the warmth of the sun, we learn to obey Him because we love Him.

Loving Him allows us to walk in triumph as we grow to know God in an intimate way, spreading the fragrance of His knowledge all around us as we go. Rejoice in this knowledge as you embark upon this journey. It's your time to *Smile, Laugh, and Be Happy!*

Scriptures: Genesis 2:16-17, 3:6-27; Matthew 4:1-11, Acts 10:38, Matthew 5:16, 1John 1:9, 2Timothy 1:14, 1John 4:12-13, 2Corinthians 2:14-15

SIGNATURE KEY

God Is On My Side!

"The Lord is on my side; I will not fear. What can man do to me?" Psalm 118:6 AMPC

ISN'T IT FUNNY THAT THE world is only familiar with *Acts of God* in terms of earthquakes, hurricanes, tornados, tsunamis, and other natural disasters? Contrary to what people may think, God is not seeking to destroy your life.

He loves you and wants to lead you to peaceful places and victorious living. The realization that God is on your side is the signature key in this wondrous, adventurous journey toward joy and happiness.

God wants us to know His true acts and share them within our sphere of influence. His acts of kindness, deliverance, provision, healing, and goodness are essential to victorious living. God wants you to know that Satan is the enemy of humanity.

The Spirit of the Living God works in and through us who belong to Him; inspiring victory, joy, love, peace, prosperity, health, happiness, wisdom, knowledge, understanding, and well-being.

Satan, the accuser of the people of God, is in opposition to everything that is righteousness, peace, and joy. He wants to work through you to promote every kind of evil in your life and the lives of others.

This includes every work of the flesh. Fear, poverty, lack, misery, sickness, death, sadness, sorrow, pride, grief, bitterness, unforgiveness, rebellion, compromise, and self- destruction have no place in your life.

What is surprising is how many times we fail to realize that the flesh and blood struggles that ensue in the earthly realm originate from the spiritual realm. In other words, many of your negative thoughts derive from a spiritual source. You will experience challenges to your personal happiness while you live on this earth.

There is no equality between God and the accuser. God is our Creator. Satan is a created being, a fallen spirit, and a defeated adversary. Once you become clear on this you will not be surprised that the battles that occur in your thought life are actually spiritual influences.

We can actually win our fight more easily than we realize when we remember that the war is in the spirit, not with other people. When you choose to meet the challenges with faith in God, you will also experience His victory. He is the Helper that assists and equips you to overcome every single time.

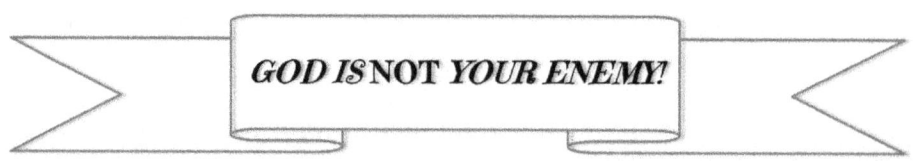

GOD IS NOT YOUR ENEMY!

He is the Friend that sticks closer than a brother. People and events may seem to work against you, but God is on your side. He says so in His word. Every day that you live you can relax in the truth that God is for you. He loves and watches over you personally, so who can triumph against you?

Absolutely no one and nothing, because no one can triumph over God! Since no one can triumph over Him, regardless of how things appear to be, you can choose to reject and overcome every offense! No one can triumph over you when you choose to be an overcomer.

The economy may seem shaky, times may appear uncertain; people around you may gripe, complain, or be hurtful and unhappy. But you are able to overcome the challenges that rise against you with the assurance that God lives within you.

What is impossible for you to do alone is possible with Him, because that which is impossible for man is possible with God.

In fact, your choice to be joy-filled and happy amid uncertain times will have a significant effect on the people that you are around daily. God put you on earth for such a time as this, so whatever you face is something you can and are to conquer. You have the power and the right to choose to perceive things as they really are. Deception, temporary setbacks, and lying vanities.

You are stronger than you think. You were born to overcome.

Aren't you glad to be alive? Doesn't it cheer your heart to realize that God is really in you and on your side? This is good news. I want you to really, really realize that being born from above means that not only is He on your side, but He also lives in you. This means that the one who is Greater than all that you face in this life is always with you.

The decision to live a life of joy and happiness in Him is yours to make. He is your Helper, the One that enables you to walk through trials and challenges, knowing that you do not face any circumstance on your own.

God is your Father, Deliverer, and greatest Advocate. He will never leave you or abandon you. Never, Ever, Ever.

Scriptures: Matthew 13:39, Ephesians 6:12, 2 Corinthians 10:3-5, Proverbs 18:24, Romans 8:28-31, Psalm 91,, Matthew 19:26, Mark 10:27, Luke 18:27, Jonah 2:8-9, Psalm 31:6-8, John 16:33, 1John 4:4, Hebrews 13:5-6

Happy Facts

1. The foundational happy key for my adventurous, victorious life is that God is personally on my side! (Psalm 118:6)

2. God is not mad at me, nor is He my enemy. (Romans 8:31)

3. God is rooting for me to live an overcoming lifestyle. (Psalm 35:27)

4. Because I am alive on earth, I will experience challenges to my personal happiness. But because of my seat in Christ, I always win. (Psalm 73:3, Psalm 18:29, 2Corinthians 2:14)

5. As an overcomer, I challenge the challenges of my life. (John 16:33)

6. There isn't anything or anyone that can keep me down because I make the decision that I will rise up and only allow joy to permeate my soul. (Luke 11:22)

7. I don't have to be an overnight faith sensation; I just continue to be consistent and faithful in exercising my faith. (Romans 10:17)

8. As I grow in these truths, I continually overcome every

challenge that comes my way. (Genesis 49:19)

My Happy Declarations

1. I am not alone. God is with me, and He will never forsake me. (Hebrews 13:5)

2. God is not my enemy; He is the Friend that sticks closer than a father, mother, brother, sister, husband, wife, or anyone else. (Proverbs 18:24)

3. It doesn't matter who or what might oppose me. I can overcome the challenges in my life because I know that God is for me. (Romans 8:31)

4. My choice to be happy and joyful in the midst of uncertain times will positively affect the people that are around me.

5. I am never alone. The Greater One lives in me. (1John 4:4)

6. I am glad and joyously alive, because God is on my side! In fact, I'm going to say it again: *"I'm glad to be alive, because God is on my side!"*

7. Now that's something to *Smile, Laugh, and Be Happy* about!

Joy Keystone

"So, what do you think? With God on our side like this, how can we lose?" Romans 8:31 TMB

"What then shall we say to [all] this? If God is for us, who [can be] against us? [Who can be our foe, if God is on our side?]" Romans 8:31 AMPC

HAPPY KEY #1

I Am One of a Kind, For God's Own Purpose!

PREACHERS, TEACHERS, SCIENTISTS, AND OTHERS have pointed it out that no two sets of fingerprints are alike. Medical and mental health professionals, as well as scientists might chime in to add that while individuals may display similar behavioral traits, in reality, no two people are exactly the same, not even "identical" multiple birth siblings.

It's not just our fingerprints that are different. Our eyes, nose, teeth, lips, ears, and many more functions and a variety of things. Our tastes buds differ, our handwriting differs, our temperaments and brains process ideals, principles, and experiences in distinctive ways.

Each of us is unique, separate and diverse, original creations of our Creator. He looks at you through everlasting, love-filled eyes. To God you are the beautifully unique individual person He created you to be.

And to make sure that He never misses out on a single eternal moment with you, He made it so that you could have a personal Father-Son relationship with Him through Jesus Christ, the One who died and rose for all mankind, which you and I are a part of. So that you could be forever with the Father.

Never compare yourself to others. You fail miserably every time you attempt to copy anyone else. That's because you are not a clone, you are an original. Even if you shared the womb with siblings, you are still an individual.

Regardless of the number of people that may have shared that womb with you, God still regards you as significant in His plan. Meditate on the word *created*. It speaks to works of art, original inventions and something unique. Be happy to be the original design that you are. Consider these statements:

"I will praise You, for I am fearfully and wonderfully made; Marvelous are Your works, And that my soul knows very well." Psalm 139:14

"For we are God's masterpiece. He has created us anew in Christ Jesus, so we can do the good things he planned for us long ago." Ephesians 2:10 NLT

Can you imagine how silly it appears in the eyes of the Creator and the angels to see His fearfully and wonderfully made humanity strive to establish superiority over one another? We're all unique originals, so why waste time trying to outdo one another when all derive from the same Creator? It's comparing what He made to what He made. Who gets to say that one person is better than another? We are designed to work together, not in opposition.

When the temptation to find fault with your body, skin color, blemishes, hair, ears, nose, talents, perfections, imperfections, gifts, abilities and other parts of yourself comes, STOP! Those thoughts and ideas are not what God says about you!

It is indeed foolish to find fault when He made you to be uniquely who you are. God created you with your own set of dreams and aspirations. It is important to Him for you to live the unique life that He designed you for.

Are you starting to believe how personal and great God's love and thoughts are just for you?

Just think; humans are the most marvelous of all of God's creations. Our very existence is one of the greatest marvels of the ages. In fact, the psalmist looked up at the vast beauty of the moon and stars and questioned the significance of humanity. He humbly penned the question, *"What is man…?"* The New Living Translation puts it this way:

> *"…what are people that you should think about them, mere mortals that you should care for them? Yet you made them only a little lower than God and crowned them with glory and honor. You gave them charge of everything you made, putting all things under their authority…" Psalm 8:4-6 NLT*

He's talking about you and me in that scripture. We are so significant to God that He made us only a little lower than He is. He made us to have dominion and rule over the works of His hands. That includes our own self-will. He didn't make us to find fault with ourselves and one another.

Instead, we can express gratitude and appreciation for life.

He didn't make us to place the greatest emphasis on physical beauty, intelligence, financial worth or social status. How sad and easily deceived we are when we allow ourselves to believe that our God-given attributes exalt or diminish the value, worth, and beauty of another human being. Now be happy that you don't do that.

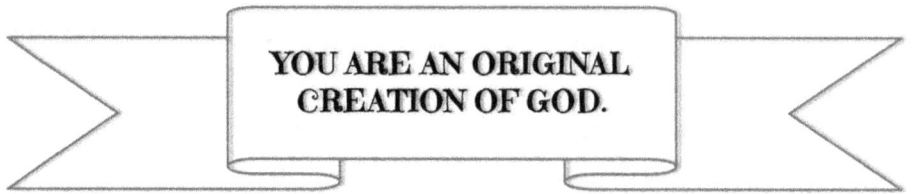

YOU ARE AN ORIGINAL CREATION OF GOD.

God made each of us to please Himself *and* to meet the needs of those around us. He wants to teach each of us how to bring forth our own true beauty and worth in this world. Our Father wants you to recognize the value that He has placed upon you. He wants you to live a significant life for Him, one that establishes your fingerprint, your laughter, your own unique signature.

He wants you to live a significant life for Him, one that establishes your fingerprint, your laughter, your own unique signature. We are all to be musical frequencies that blend as part of His choir of love, joy, peace, salvation, healing and goodness on this earth. Be what God created you to be. He has great plans for your life.

Think Yourself Beautiful.
Think Yourself Happy.
Be HIS Masterpiece!

Scriptures: 1Corinthians 12, Jeremiah 29:11, Philippians 4:8-9

Happy Facts

1. True beauty is not an outside thing, it is a God thing.

2. I don't need makeovers of any kind. God did it right the first time. I am beautiful [handsome, gorgeous, stunning] and happy. I am one fine-looking example of God's artistry. (Ephesians 2:10)

3. I am fearfully and wonderfully made, a wonderful work of God. (Psalm 139:14)

4. My creativity, laughter, fingerprints and expressions of joy are part of my personal life signature.

5. God placed me into this earth to accomplish something for His Kingdom that is unique to me, and I'm doing it. (Romans 8:28 ASV)

6. I will not give my attention to what Hollywood, Madison Avenue, friends or family says about my life if it is contrary to the word of God. Jesus said it all with His Blood. That makes me priceless. (1 John 2:2)

7. God gave me His Spirit, so with His help I will discover the importance He places upon my life and live it out. (Psalm 8, John 14:26, 16:13)

8. I have a reason to sing happy songs to Him, because no one else in this entire world is just like me. I am one of a kind, for

God's own purpose. (Ephesians 1:11,12)

My Happy Declarations

1. I will not allow society or another person's opinion of beauty or success to exalt, devalue or diminish me. God is leading me to triumph in all that I do. I'm perfect **for my purpose —God** said so. I believe Him and this makes me happy. (2 Corinthians 2:14)

2. God put me here to work with others. I am God's field, He is building me. (1 Corinthians 3:1-9)

3. I was created to introduce hope to others. I am in the earth to inspire joy and happiness in others, just by being the person God created me to be. (Acts 17:28)

4. God has given me His breath of life so that I can walk with Him in the cool of the day and discover the value He places upon my life. (Genesis 2:7 NIV)

5. My dreams and aspirations are unique to me. My life is important to the Lord. He has great plans for me. (Jeremiah 29:11)

6. The Creator of the universe is teaching me how to bring forth my true beauty and worth to this world. I have my own fingerprint, my own laugh, my own unique signature. There really is no one else in the world that is just like me. (Psalm 139:14, Ephesians 2:10)

7. I am one of a kind, for God's purpose. (Philippians 1:6)

8. This prosperity of soul gives me a real reason to *Smile, Laugh and Be Happy!*

Joy Keystone

"For You shaped me, inside and out. You knitted me together in my mother's womb long before I took my first breath. 14 I will offer You my grateful heart, for I am Your unique creation, filled with wonder and awe. You have approached even the smallest details with excellence; Your works are wonderful; I carry this knowledge deep within my soul."

Psalm 139:13-14 VOICE

A Few Things To Think About...

Do you realize that you are blessed by God? Has it ever occurred to you that God's original design for you includes His intent to spend time with you, provide for you, and continually bless you? Selah (stop, think and meditate on these truths).

Even after Adam's sin in the Garden of Eden, God remained faithful to create ways to restore relationship and provide for His beloved creation. You are not less valuable, no matter what you have done. Genesis 1:26 clearly states that you are God's creation.

> *"Beloved, I pray that you may prosper in all things and be in health, just as your soul prospers." 3 John 2-3*

Say this aloud: *"It pleases God to prosper me in my soul and my body."*

When I read and meditate every day upon God's word, I fill my mind with the ability to think happy. God's word originates from the way that He thinks. Happy thoughts originate with God's Word.

> *"For my thoughts are not your thoughts, neither are your ways My ways, says the Lord." Isaiah 55:8*

In light of what Isaiah says, answer these simple questions for yourself:

A. When I think and confess happy thoughts, then I align my thinking and my actions with the word of God. *Who am I thinking like and agreeing with?*

B. When I think and confess defeat and discouragement,

then I align my thinking and actions with the god of this world. *Who am I thinking like and agreeing with?*

Do you know how much God wants you to be happy? If you aren't sure, just look at the fact that He has appointed the Feast of Tabernacles, one of the High Holy Days, specifically as a day for joy and happiness.

Even though we don't celebrate in that manner anymore, these Holy days are still His idea. This joy and happiness will even continue in the millennium. Jesus went to this joyous feast and provided a way for you to do likewise in Him.

Let the good times of refreshing in Him roll you right past the worries and cares of the day! Better than Mardi Gras, God's days of joy and happiness can occur every day of your life.

Scriptures: Leviticus 23:34, Deuteronomy 16:13, John 7:2, Acts 3:19

A Joy Key From God's Word

Imagine yourself in the face of simple everyday adversities like a dead car battery or flat tire, a traffic jam, or a missed flight, bus, or train. Many people, including Believers, Christians, and even some Kingdom folk would gripe and complain about the situation. But not you. No, you will laugh, allowing the joy of the Lord to change your atmosphere.

"Me? Laugh at this stuff? Really?"

Yes, you do! Now that's a radically defiant position against Satan's kingdom and its order. Nevertheless, this is our warfare posture. We face down everything that comes against us clothed in joy!

> *"My fellow believers, when it seems as though you are facing nothing but difficulties see it as an invaluable opportunity to experience the greatest joy that you can! 3For you know that when your faith is tested it stirs up power within you to endure all things. 4 And then as your endurance grows even stronger it will release perfection into every part of your being until there is nothing missing and nothing lacking. "*
> *James 1:2-4 TPT*

God's word says to count it all joy, so do what He says, because the very laughter that you release into situations such as these releases you into victory in the spirit realm. Laughter is a medicine as well as a spiritual weapon; a laser sword, a brilliant light that paralyzes the power of darkness.

Laughter and praise will rout the demonic out of place. It renders demons ineffective in your life. Laughter is a shout! A sign of Victory. The kingdom of darkness experiences a crushing defeat as our submission to God's word forces them to retreat.

Toxic thoughts, complaints, bitterness, fear, and other negatives are works of the flesh. You have no time for depression! You're too busy releasing the spirit of joy and praise into the atmosphere.

Keep laughing and praising the Lord. It works for your good.

> *"At destruction and famine thou shalt laugh: neither shalt thou be afraid of the beasts of the earth." Job 5:22*
>
> *"Out of the mouth of babes and nursing infants You have ordained strength, Because of Your enemies, That You may silence the enemy and the avenger." Psalm 8:2*
>
> *"Then was our mouth filled with laughter, and our tongue with singing: then said they among the heathen, The Lord hath done great things for them. 3The Lord hath done great things for us; whereof we are glad." Psalm 126:2-3 KJV*
>
> *"Always be glad because of the Lord! I will say it again: Be glad." Philippians 4:4 CEV*
>
> *He who sits [enthroned] in the heavens laughs [at their rebellion]; The [Sovereign] Lord scoffs at them [and in supreme contempt He mocks them]. Psalm 2:4 AMPC*

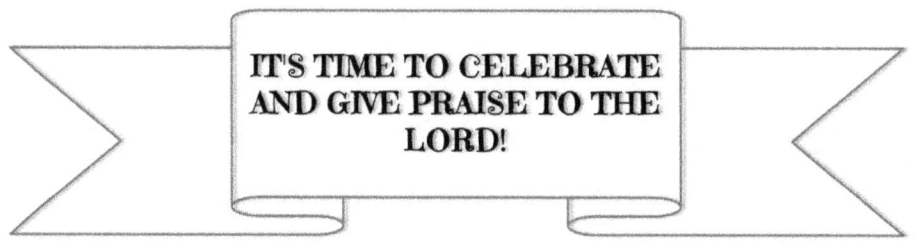

VICTORY SHOUT SONG

Words by Lonzine Lee
Can be sung to the tune of "The Hokey Pokey"

I speak the Word of God, I say it to myself

I speak the Word of God, And I give my brain a rest.

I've put my trust in Someone, Who knows me inside out,

So I let out a victory shout (Yeah!)

I put the good thoughts in, I speak the good words out.

I put the good thoughts in, Then I start
to laugh at doubt. (Ha! Ha!)

I do a little shuffle

And I dance around a lot,

Then I let out a victory shout. (Yeah!)

Ha-Ha. Ha-Ha. Ha-Ha.

Ha-Ha. Ha-Ha. He-He.

Ha-Ha. Ha-Ha. Ha-Ha.

I really have to laugh at doubt. (He-he)
'Cause I've put my trust in Jesus.

He has turned my thoughts around,

So I let out a victory shout, Oh yeah!

I let out a victory shout!

YEAH!

HAPPY KEY #2

God Gave Me The Power To Choose My Thoughts

YOUR THOUGHT LIFE CREATES THE vision that helps determine your direction and choice for happiness. According to God, contentment is not measured by how others treat or think about us. That's a self-absorbed kind of life. Who is the Source of our personal happiness? The Spirit of God Himself. The Word of God declares that happiness is found in how we treat and think about self and others. That leads to selfless or "self-ish" living.

It is common in our society for people to place the responsibility for their joy and happiness on others. Some fail to take on their own identity through feeding the want or need to be entertained, pampered; even live virtually through the efforts of someone else. Whether it's a mate, sports event, a movie, television, books, music, or role-playing games, bring on the show! And this very habit of catering to suggestive emotional needs and desires can override the desire for Truth.

That's even true about church. The preacher, soloist, choir, song service, etc. must meet personal standards of enjoyment in alignment with secular standards of pleasure, or it's too boring to deal with. Church is expected to comply with Hollywood and/or socially acceptable standards on how to preach the right message, hold the right length of service, and so on.

Suddenly, God's messengers are put on a poll chart comparing popularity and relevancy. Leaders are expected to do all they can to please or cater to the whims of "the people" if what they do is to be judged as acceptable.

This is so demonic.

Have you ever seen a film or television show where character fantasizes about escaping to a private island? Here they will recline in luxury, away from all the cares of life while attractive minions feed them grapes and rich delicacies.

They imagine themselves resting in shaded luxury, a tropical beverage of choice within reach, while fawning servants fan their faces with large palm fronds; eager to make sure that they do whatever it takes to please the master or mistress.

Some unhappy, self-absorbed, or even narcissistic people mistreat spouses, children, parents, co-workers, friends, preachers, and even God in the manner of an entitled, self-centered brat. Since they can't have their way, they will try to dictate. *"Your only purpose in my life is to entertain me and to do what I want you to do and make me happy!"*

Ha-Ha. They think that this is the good life that they deserve, a life where others serve them. But look at what King Solomon had to say:

> *"I've decided that there's nothing better to do than go ahead and have a good time and get the most we can out of life. That's it — eat, drink, and make the most of your job. It's God's gift."* Ecclesiastes 3:12-13 ESV

King Solomon truly knew what living a privileged, lavish lifestyle entailed. He knew firsthand what it was like to enjoy any type of pleasure he desired. Yet, in this writing he favors a lifestyle that is not subject to always requires others to cater to his whims.

Instead, it is a life of gratitude, and enjoyment of the privilege to have a life filled with adventure, laughter, entertainment, and so forth because life is a gift from God. He lived and learned the vanity of self-indulgence.

Selfish striving to get your own way does not allow you to live with true happiness, nor does it lead to mature faith or victorious living. It is an indicator that you are being self-centered. It may please you temporarily, but it isn't a useful trait, and it surely puts a strain on your interpersonal relationships. True joy does not come from flesh. True joy comes from the Spirit of the Fear of the God. So, what is the source of the thoughts that characterize *your* lifestyle?

Remember, God wants you to have His joy, the unselfish kind! The journey to joy will lead you through struggles and challenges, which are necessary in order to have mature faith. When I say that the journey to joy will lead you through, I mean that you will experience struggles and challenges to your faith, but you won't live in that land forever. As you think on what God has said and promised, the pure joy of the Lord will lead the way in and the way out of each challenge.

> "Consider it pure joy, my brothers, whenever you face trials of many kinds, because you know that the testing of your faith develops perseverance. Perseverance must finish its work so that you may be mature and complete, not lacking anything." James 1:2-4 NIV

Do you have to *feel* happy in order to be happy? It helps, but it is not essential. Your feelings can lead you, but they will most likely deceive you and lead you to a place that you don't really want to go. True happiness is a deliberate choice; a joyous and decisive act of your will to think and be happy despite all the opportunities to feel something else. As you practice doing the hard things with your thoughts centered on God's promises, you will attain success because you are being led by the Spirit of God.

Your success will build confidence within you. As you change, so will your thoughts. Your thoughts will lead your feelings. *"To be or not to be,"* may be the question according to William Shakespeare, but according to God, *"To Feel or To Be"* is your decision. You are strong and smart enough to avoid the demonic *"Me-Me-Me"* song of selfishness.

You can follow your heart (kardia in the Greek), but that's just a fancy way of saying that you are meditating on your thoughts or feelings. In this sense, following your heart or emotions spoils you for the uncommon goodness of God. Jesus spoke about that possibility,

> *"...But the words you speak come from the heart—that's what defiles you. For from the heart come evil thoughts, murder, adultery, all sexual immorality, theft, lying, and slander. These are what defile you." Matthew 15:18-20*

The word "defile" basically means "to make common." In other words, you can live a regular fleshly life just like most people do. People that live according to the flesh pay a great price for living according to their feelings and emotions, but not you, becayse you do not live according to the flesh. Hear this truth: You have the right to choose to live contrary to the fleshly, touchy, feely, common way of life.

If you want to be happy, you can be happy. You do not have to feel it first. If you want to laugh aloud, you can laugh aloud. You do not have to be entertained before you laugh. If you want to rejoice when everything around you looks like it's falling apart, you can rejoice. Circumstances cannot stop you.

You have the joy of the Lord! You don't owe your flesh any obligation to feel sad, mad, gloomy or depressed! You have the power to choose the thoughts and actions of God, and no one in this earth can stop you.

You know that there is something better to do than to try and get the most out of life. You are vitally connected to the True Vine, the true source of a victorious, joyous life. All you have to do is ask Him to lead you into the life He has for you, and He will do it.

You are happy and you know it, so be bold, go forth and show it. Now that's living! See, you have another reason to *Smile, Laugh and Be Happy!*

Scriptures: Nehemiah 8:10, Romans 8:12-13, John 15:1

Happy Facts

1. Yay! I can be happy if I want to be, and nobody can stop me.

2. I have the power to override my own negative thoughts, so I will act on that now.

3. I reign over my thoughts, mind and body. I am powerful. (Romans 8:1)

4. I do not have to live and act according to my negative feelings, so I don't. (Romans 8:12 AMPC)

5. I don't limit my vision to what I can see. I see what God has said. I choose to be joyful when the circumstances try to dictate that I be sad, fearful and unhappy. This makes me glad. (2 Corinthians 4:18)

6. Circumstances do not order my thinking or my mood, I do. (James 1:2 ESV)

7. When I think and confess happy thoughts, I align myself with God's plans for me.

8. I believe that "God said and it was so." That's my tool for being obedient and blessed in my thinking. (Genesis 1)

9. Since I can dictate my own thinking; I can decide my attitude. I now make the decision to change my attitude and to be happy. (Philippians 4:8)

My Happy Declarations

1. I do not have to feel happy to be happy. I am happy because I choose to be. My feelings will catch up with my decision. Like the Apostle Paul, I can think myself happy. (Acts 26:2)

2. I am strong and filled with the joy of the Lord. (Nehemiah 8:10)

3. I have the power to choose my own thoughts. I am not in debt to my emotions. (Romans 8:12)

4. No one has to entertain me to get me to smile. Laughter flows from within my belly like living water. (John 7:38)

Joy Keystone

"So we are convinced that every detail of our lives is continually woven together to fit into God's perfect plan of bringing good into our lives, for we are His lovers who have been called to fulfill His designed purpose." **TPT**

And we know that all things work together for good to those who love God, to those who are the called according to His purpose....NKJV

We are confident that God is able to orchestrate everything to work toward something good and beautiful when we love Him and accept His invitation to live according to His plan." VOICE

Romans 8:28 **TPT** - NKJV - **VOICE**

Today I Pray...

Lord, it is my desire to align my thoughts and my ways with You.

I commit and entrust my thoughts, actions and deeds entirely to You, so that my thoughts become agreeable to Your will; and so that my plans and my actions are established and rooted in Your word and I succeed in all that I endeavor to do.

Instruct me on how to trust You, laugh, and count it all joy when I am faced with adverse and frightening circumstances. Lead me to learn how to reject fear when my eyes and ears are confronted with lack and destruction. I choose to agree with You for my salvation and safety. Open my eyes so that I see that there are more with me than there are against me. I choose to believe You and I want my life to reflect my choice.

When difficulty comes my way, I know that I do not face it alone. Thank You for always being with me, even when I don't feel Your Presence. Thank You for giving me the desires of Your heart for me, and for the fulfilling of every yes and amen promise that is in You. O Lord, I put my trust in You. I know that I am safe with You. In Jesus' Name, Amen.

Scriptures: Joshua 1:8, 2 Kings 6:16-17, 2Chronicles 4:10, 32:7, Psalm 7:1, Psalm 16:1, Psalm 25:20, Psalm 31:1, Psalm 56:11, Psalm 71:1, Proverbs 16:3 AMPC
Jeremiah 20:11, James 1:2-4

HAPPY KEY #3
A Grateful Heart Stills Fear

"This is the day the Lord has made; We will rejoice and be glad in it." Psalm 118:24

HAVE YOU BLESSED THE LORD FOR TODAY? A heart that is continually thankful keeps the channels of love and communication open between the Creator and His creation, and it keeps your lips from uttering words of complaint, defeat, poverty, lack, fear, doubt, offense or unforgiveness.

Today is a beautiful day. I can say this because my Bible tells me that the Lord made the day for me to rejoice and be glad. Each new dawn brings new opportunities, possibilities and reasons to be glad. He even provides us with new mercies, unfailing compassion and great faithfulness.

Having a grateful heart is necessary in order to maintain victory in any given situation, because a heart of gratitude continually recognizes God as the Giver of all the good things worth having in this life.

Think about it. If you are constantly thanking God for who He is, and who He is in your life, when do you have time to worry? Gratitude keeps you from worrying, because your heart knows and remembers that the same God that delivered you once will do it again and again and again.

If you are not worrying, you have peace. If you are at peace, you are not in a state of worry; you are not fearful or concerned about the circumstances of your life. You are doing what Matthew 6:31-33 says:

> "Therefore do not worry, saying, 'What shall we eat?' or 'What shall we drink?' or 'What shall we wear?' For after all these things the Gentiles seek. For your heavenly Father knows that you need all these things. But seek first the kingdom of God and His righteousness, and all these things shall be added to you."

It's amazing how often fear and doubt cause the air to be polluted with the unpleasant odor of complaints and criticisms of unhappy, unforgiving, unrepentant, bitter, and sad people. Focusing on the past, they become unhappy. They don't expect God's love and goodness to manifest. When it does, they are afraid to be happy because *"it won't last."*

This is the perfect setup for increased misery. But the Bible says that it is good to give God thanks and to sing His praises.

> *"It is good to give thanks to the Lord, And to sing praises to Your name, O Most High; To declare Your lovingkindness in the morning, And Your faithfulness every night..."* Psalm 92:1-2

God gave you the same ability that He Himself has, to be able to declare a thing and have it be established for you. You have the authority to help change the atmosphere with your words. What you speak into the earth makes an impact and a difference in your life and the lives of the people around you.

Do you realize that you can refresh the air simply by releasing words of praise, gratitude and thanksgiving? Rejoice in the love and goodness of the Lord.

When you do, you radiate joy and light, and it affects the very air that you breathe. As you allow happiness to flow from you, you exert the power and strength that comes from the joy of the Lord. This causes the darkness around you to scatter, because you have called upon your Deliverer.

King David even wrote a song after God delivered him from a dark situation. One of the things that he says is that when He called upon the Lord, He came down, and darkness was under His feet!

> *"In my distress I called upon the Lord, and cried out to my God; He heard my voice from His temple, And my cry came before Him, even to His ears. Then the earth shook and trembled; The foundations of the hills also quaked and were shaken, Because He was angry. Smoke went up from His nostrils, And devouring fire from His mouth; Coals were kindled by it. He bowed the heavens also, and came down With darkness under His feet." Psalm 18:6-9*

That's right, when you choose to be joyous and happy, **darkness flees!** Whenever you call upon the Lord, He shows up, and darkness must bow. In this same psalm, David later goes on and proclaims,

> *"You will light my lamp; The Lord my God will enlighten my darkness. By You I can run against a troop, By my God I can leap over a wall. As for God, His way is perfect; The word of the Lord is proven; He is a shield to all who trust in Him." Psalm 18:28-30*

Learn what it means to live in God's secret place. Here's a clue. *Read, meditate, study,* and *remember Psalm 91.* God's word is our shelter, a refuge and a fortress that protects us from everything Satan has in his arsenal. In God's secret place, light overcomes darkness. Joy triumphs over sorrow. Gratitude defeats negativity.

In Him, we have everything that we need to overcome. Gratitude activates the resources of God's kingdom. Faith activates His power. Remember, it is a good thing to give God thanks. It is a beneficial to bless His name.

> *"I will bless the Lord who has given me counsel; My heart also instructs me in the night seasons. I have set the Lord always before me; Because He is at my right hand I shall not be moved. Therefore my heart is glad, and my glory rejoices; My flesh also will rest in hope." Psalm 16:7-9*

True gratitude prohibits dissatisfaction from gaining hold upon your thinking. In fact, when your mind is continuously in the habit of counting your blessings, *your mouth* is continuously in the habit of speaking about the blessings of God. Out of the abundance of gratitude in your heart your mouth will speak. Become abundant in your gratitude and you will have a change of attitude. You will have no problem speaking about God's goodness.

What can you thank Him for?

Thank Him For His Goodness.
Thank Him For His Provision And Faithfulness.
Thank Him For A New Attitude And Outlook On Life.
Thank Him For Joy And Laughter Overflowing Within.
Thank Him For Salvation and His Mercy.
Thank Him for your breath. You are still alive.

Yes, Thank God For His Mercy!

"Bless our God, O peoples, give Him grateful thanks and make the voice of His praise be heard, Who put and kept us among the living, and has not allowed our feet to slip." Psalm 66:8-9 AMPC

Answer these questions about yourself for yourself: *How clean and fresh is the air around you?* Are you thankful for what God has done in and for you? *Do you know that He is capable of blessing you in the midst of an unstable economy?* Will you choose to be glad when you are tempted to be mad or sad about your circumstances?

If your answer to those questions is *"Yes,"* then you have *chosen to be* a winner. So do I. And in this moment, I choose to laugh out loud! Join me.

Now is a good time to give Him thanks, because you honestly have something to rejoice, *Smile, Laugh and Be Happy* about!

Scriptures: Colossians 3:8, 1 John 4:18, Lamentations 3:22-23, Nehemiah 8:10, 2 Samuel 22, Psalm 18, Job 22:28, Luke 6:45

Happy Facts

1. I purify the air around me by speaking words of joy, gladness, forgiveness, encouragement and gratitude. (Psalm 92:10)

2. When I have unhappy people around me, I will allow the joy of the Lord within me to diffuse the air I breathe and give them hope. If they reject it, then I will take my joy someplace else. (Isaiah 51:11)

3. Expressing gratitude in the midst of my trouble is an exercise of my faith in El-Shaddai; The God Who is Sufficient [More Than Enough] for the needs of His people. That's faith in action. (Isaiah 65:19, James 2:21-26)

4. My willingness to express gratitude toward God in less than ideal circumstances shows my love and trust for Him, and is an act of obedience that brings me blessing. (Jeremiah 31:13)

5. It makes no sense to be mad or sad when I remember that He makes me glad, so I rejoice! (Psalm 32:11)

6. I am willing and obedient to be grateful to God, so I will eat the best of the land. (Isaiah 1:19)

7. I pay attention to what God says, so I am blessed everywhere that I go, and in all that I do. (Deuteronomy 28:1-14)

8. I thank You, Lord, I thank You, Lord. I'm blessed! I'm blessed! I'm blessed! (Psalm 26:7)

My Happy Declarations

1. Since I'm grateful and I know it, I speak and show it!

2. I cultivate the fragrance that accompanies faith, gratitude and joy.

3. Gratitude perfumes my atmosphere and brings blessings. (Philippians 4:18-19)

4. The more I increase in gratitude, the better my attitude.

5. Gratitude prohibits dissatisfaction from dominating my thoughts.

6. My mind and my mouth continuously speak about the blessings of God.

7. I am thankful for all that God does for me.

Joy Keystone

"Blessed are those who make You their strength, for they treasure *every step of* the journey [to Zion]. ⁶ On their way through the valley of Baca, they *stop and* dig wells to collect *the refreshing* spring water, and the early rains fill the pools. ⁷ They journey from place to place, gaining strength *along the way;* until they meet God in Zion."

Psalm 84:5-7 VOICE

HAPPY KEY #4
A Merry Heart is Good for My Health and My Wealth

"Then Abraham fell upon his face, and laughed, and said in his heart, Shall a child be born unto him that is an hundred years old? and shall Sarah, that is ninety years old, bear?" Genesis 17:17

D O YOU HAVE YET-TO-BE REALIZED promises and dreams from days that seem long ago? You may have had dreams or promises of health, wealth, a happy marriage, a thriving ministry, friendships, children, college education, travel, and so on. These are the kind of things that made you happy in the beginning, just thinking about what God has promised you.

Now, because so much time has passed since you first received the promise, the hopes and dreams may barely seem alive. Admittedly you sometimes think that you are too old or you wonder, *"Has God forgotten me? Can I really marry now? Does anyone even want me? Why hasn't it happened for me yet?"*

Why continue to believe God when the most practical time

for His promise to happen for you is come and gone? That's how Abraham and Sarah may have felt after so many years without seeing God's promise of a child manifest. Abraham had a son in his old age, but Ishmael wasn't the *promised* child. *Sarah* is the woman that God said would birth the child of promise. Not Hagar.

Undoubtedly, Abraham had the opportunity to wonder just how many more years would pass before the promise would come, if it ever came at all. It simply did not seem possible for them to have a child together, especially since Sarah was not just barren, but was well past menopause. This is the situation Sarah found herself in when she discovered at the age of 90 that she was to give birth to a child.

She knew that her husband was capable of fathering a child, but for her the hopes of motherhood were very dim. At least, that's what she felt and thought until God spoke within her hearing.

"And Sarah said, God hath made me to laugh, so that all that hear will laugh with me." Genesis 21:6

And as Sarah laughed, she opened herself to receive the faith that led to the manifestation of the promise of God.

"By faith Sarah herself also received strength to conceive seed, and she bore a child when she was past the age, because she judged Him faithful who had promised." Hebrews 11:11

You may very well have settled into a life of resignation and disappointment.

But God never told you to give up!

> "I wait for the Lord, my soul waits, And in His word I do hope." Psalm 130:5

This may sound ridiculous to you if it looks like God has forgotten you. You may feel or believe that you are too old [and tired] to succeed today; you'd be competing with younger, fresher talent. But God finds a purpose for the young *and* the old.

Don't give up! God specializes in the impossibilities of life. *"Ha! Ha! Ha!"* laughs God. He is not daunted by the limitations of the times, body clocks, calendars, medical suppositions or opinions of mankind.

Consider the evidence. Nothing, not even your chronological earth age is a disadvantage to God. *It is what you think* about your age that causes you problems. *This is your time.* Now is your time to learn to *laugh with God* and like Sarah, open yourself up to the new life that He has for you.

Read Deuteronomy 17:8 and Genesis 18, then answer the question, *"Is anything too hard for my God?"* **NO!**

> "For still the vision awaits its appointed time; it hastens to the end—it will not lie. If it seems slow, wait for it; it will surely come; it will not delay." Habakkuk 2:3 ESV

Remember, regardless of what people or circumstances may say; God keeps His promises! Truly that is a reason for your *Smile, Laugh and Be Happy* season!

Scriptures: Genesis 15:4, 17:1-19; Galatians 4:28, Luke 1:37, Psalm 2:2-4, Proverbs 16:31, 23:7a, Hebrews 11:11, 2Corinthians 1:18-20, Galatians 6:9, 2Thessalonians 3:13, Hebrews 12:3

Happy Facts

1. Happiness propels me to the place of manifestation.

2. The goodness of God leads me away from doubt and unbelief, which is sin. (Romans 2:4)

3. God is not limited by time — past, present or future. (Revelation 1:8)

4. My age is not a detriment to God's plans for me. (Proverbs 16:31, Jeremiah 1:6-7)

5. God's promises to me are still alive in me. (2 Corinthians 1:20)

6. My dreams are not dead. They were just dry. I am watering them with His word now. (Proverbs 13:12b)

7. There is nothing and no one in my life that is too difficult for my Lord to handle. (Genesis 18:14)

8. Ha! Ha! Ha! Because I believe and agree with Him, I can laugh with God.

My Happy Declaration

1. Ha-Ha-Ha! *This is my time.* I don't care what others think, I don't care what the calendar says. God says that my time is here, and I say it too. This is my time!

2. God has not forgotten me!

3. I will not give up my vision of His promise. It will surely come. (Habakkuk 2:3)

4. Just like Sarah, I laugh and open myself to receive the faith that leads to manifested promises. (Genesis 21:6, Hebrews 11:11)

5. As long as I choose to believe, I will receive the fulfillment of my hopes and desires in Him.

6. In Him, I can believe again, I can dream again, I can hope again. (Psalm 18:29, Hebrews 11:1)

7. Since I can, I do!

Joy Keystones

"I think myself happy..."
Apostle Paul, Acts 26:2

"Is anything too hard for the Lord? At the time appointed I will return unto thee..."
Genesis 18:14

HAPPY KEY #5

Joy Really Does Come

"...Weeping may endure for a night, but joy comes in the morning." Psalm 30:5 AMPC

THIS KEY IS A DISCUSSION REGARDING death and bereavement. It may seem strange to have this topic in a book that focuses on having joy and being happy, but spirits of death, grief, bereavement, sorrow, sadness, and fear have had too much power among God's people.

If you pause for a moment and think about the word "Death," you come to realize that people in America (and other countries) commonly refer to death, dying and killing in their speech. Think about the culture and the informal style of speech that comes from the mouths of many. People are constantly claiming that they are "scared to death." Including those in the body of Christ.

A spouse or child will be "the death of me," or you hear individuals describe someone or something that they "love to death," even as they tell you that they "died laughing" at a movie they just saw. Women wear shoes that are "to die for," and then proclaim that their murderous feet are "killing" them. And while "it kills" them to admit the truth, savvy investors will still seek to make "a killing" in the stock market.

People talk about the death of a dream or relationship, while divorce talk is the death ring of a marriage. Even some foods are in on the act. Did you know that there is a decadent cake known by the names "Death by Chocolate" and "Killer Chocolate Cake"? And of course, death is mocked, or at least portrayed in satirical films as the Grim Reaper; a silent, hooded, black-robed, skeletal, scythe-bearing figure that has come to reap the souls of humanity.

While all these expressions are woven into the pop culture, much of it revolves around emotions. By common definition, death is "the end of life or the cessation of a relationship." It is an earthly farewell to a dream, desire, lifestyle, family pet, or an individual. Death comes by many causes: natural, sickness, disease, accident or an intentional action by one or more individuals.

Regardless of how it occurs, death makes an impact on the soul (mind, will and emotions) as well as the heart of us all. So how do we deal with its impact when it comes our way?

One area we must learn to guard is our hearts. Dark emotions such as bitterness, anger, unforgiveness, hard hearts, division, gossip, complaining, fault-finding, and other such things have an origin. They are emotions that feed off of demonic conversations allowed to play in the audio channels of our thinking.

We have to rid ourselves of the willingness to entertain wrong beliefs, misconceptions, shame, and blame. The Bible teaches us that these types of attitudes are works of the flesh that we walk in but cannot use these things to overcome darkness. That is where the spirit of joy and happiness come in.

A season of mourning does not necessitate one specific type of behavior. Individuals mourn and say goodbye to loved ones in different ways, on their own emotional time schedules. There is no specific manner in which an individual will mourn the death of a family member or friend, especially when you do not understand the timing or reason for the death.

"It makes no sense, he was so young," "Why did they kill themselves? They had everything to live for?" or "Why did God let this happen? She was believing God for her healing, and she died."

"The Lord is my shepherd; I shall not want. He makes me to lie down in green pastures; He leads me beside the still waters. He restores my soul; He leads me in the paths of righteousness For His name's sake. Yea, though I walk through the valley of the shadow of death, I will fear no evil; For You are with me; Your rod and Your staff, they comfort me.

You prepare a table before me in the presence of my enemies; You anoint my head with oil; My cup runs over. Surely goodness and mercy shall follow me all the days of my life; And I will dwell in the house of the Lord forever." Psalm 23

Many times when a death happens, we have more questions than answers. It is not meant for us to immediately have all the answers that would satisfy our desire to understand. If it were, then God would have made it clear. This is an area where trust in Him is so necessary. When we trust Him, He never disappoints us. (1 Peter 2:6) He always comes through.

Remember that no matter how close we are or think that we are to another person; no one knows everything about a situation, or the true thoughts and innermost beliefs of another person. We don't have the whole story, regardless of how much they may share with us. No one but God knows all about us. Not our parents, siblings, spouses, children, or our own selves.

WHEN WE TRUST OUR HEAVENLY FATHER, HE NEVER DISAPPOINTS US!

We sometimes question ourselves about what we really believe. The only person who knows everything about us is God. With His love and care for us, He walks us through any and every situation that we encounter and leads us to a healing place. **We are supposed to overcome these spirits, not submit to them.**

So trust the One that knows you through and through. There is no doubt you will be glad that you did.

Remember God does not think of death the way we do, if we are His. Psalms 116:15 in the NIV says, *"Precious in the sight of the Lord is the death of his faithful servants."*

I want to live to complete all that He has for me and I believe that you do also. But remember it is neither your place or mine to judge why others gave up the fight or seem to have lost the battle. God is the only one that has all the answers. My joy and happiness is in the truth that I trust Him. And that makes me happy.

And also remember, He made us, we did not make Him. So trust the One that knows you through and through. There is no doubt you will be glad that you did.

Scriptures: 2Corinthians 10:3, Galatians 5:19, 1Peter 2:6

WHY WE CAN SING HAPPY SONGS...

Do you have 100 reasons to be grateful to God? Of course you do, even in the midst of grief. But do you know what those 100 reasons are? That's a different matter altogether. A grateful heart is essential in order to maintain joy and happiness. Gratitude is also a powerful weapon to use when the spirit of grief is in your atmosphere.

Every gift from God is worth pursuing. Since you know that an attitude of gratitude is worth having, practice being grateful on a daily basis.

Count your blessings the way others count their reasons for complaining. Keep a diary or a list of reasons that you have to be thankful, it will change your life. Even more, it will be a part of your joy arsenal, something that you can refer to whenever you are tempted to feel sad or unhappy.

If you practice listing a reason why you are grateful to God one day at a time for the next 30 days, you will know 30 reasons why you have something to smile, laugh and be happy about. If you do it again for another 30 days, you will have 60 reasons. If you do it again for 30 days after that, you're up to 90. And if you keep going every day for the next year, you will have 365-plus reasons to give Him praise.

Even better, every time you're tempted to complain or feel sorry for yourself, you have an internal counterattack for negativity and dark emotions. The joy of the Lord is your strength. The blessings of the Lord make you rich and do not add sorrow.

In fact, when you list one of your reasons for gratitude, give yourself an extra treat and **find a scripture reference that backs it up.** The word of the Lord is pure power, more than enough to overcome any kind of downturn, whether economic, physical, relational, medical, or emotional.

I believe in this so much, I'll even get you started on the first 30 days. Three headings, three ways to list it. I challenge you to find reasons to *Smile, Laugh and Be Happy*.

God has blessed me with…	I am grateful to God for…	I give praise to God for…
1	1	1
2	2	2
3	3	3
4	4	4
5	5	5
6	6	6
7	7	7
8	8	8
9	9	9
10	10	10

Scriptures:

Nehemiah 8:10 – *The joy of the Lord is your strength.*

Psalm 118:24 – *This is the day that the Lord has made…rejoice and be glad today.*

Proverbs 10:22 – *The blessings of the Lord make you rich…He does not add sorrow.*

Lamentations 3:22-23 – *God's faithfulness is great…His mercies are new every morning.*

1Peter 1:3-9 – *You are kept by His power…you rejoice with inexpressible joy.*

3John 4 – *It gives God great joy to see you walk in His truth.*

THE JOY OF THE LORD IS TRIUMPHANT OVER GRIEF

"To everything there is a season, and a time for every matter or purpose under heaven: A time to be born and a time to die, a time to plant and a time to pluck up what is planted, A time to kill and a time to heal, a time to break down and a time to build up, A time to weep and a time to laugh, a time to mourn and a time to dance…" Ecclesiastes 3:1-4 AMPC

SINCE THE FOCUS OF THIS BOOK is the truth that God wants you to have joy and be happy, what exactly is God's perspective when it comes to times and seasons of death and the mourning processThe Bible tells us that the death of His saints is precious to Him. That tells us that He does not see death as the end of our existence. He sees death as an absence from the human body, but we are then fully present with Him.

It speaks of rejoicing with those who rejoice and weeping with those that weep, which provides the reminder that we have seasons for both. It also speaks of weeping that endures for a night, with joy coming in the morning. This is a spiritual principle – sadness can and must be replaced with joy. Why is it so important to have joy in place of sorrow and sadness?

It is because *sadness and grief must come to an end if we are going to live life.* Morning represents fresh hope and a new start. I can imagine someone picking up this book during a time in life when laughing is the last thing that you feel like doing.

"How do you laugh when your heart grieves over the loss of a loved one? How do you rejoice when you hear of horrible deaths or tragedy somewhere else in the world? How do you smile when you feel like your heart is broken?"

God has an answer to each of those questions. Within the pages of His Holy Word you discover the truths you need as you *learn what you really believe about Him in times of trouble and heartache.* The truth is found in the character of God Himself. He is the One who promises to never leave or forsake you.

"Doesn't the Bible say to mourn with those that mourn? Is it even appropriate to laugh during times of grief or bereavement?

How do you still believe in a God that angers you because He allowed someone that you love to be taken away from you?

WHY? WHY? WHY?"

Mercifully, in spite of how you feel about it, the sorrow that you experience can be temporary. Father God is not afraid of your anger, disappointment, or even your lack of trust in Him. He wants you to give Him every overwhelming emotion, every pain, every bit of the ugliness and despair that you feel. Even what you feel toward Him. He can take it; He really is our Healer. And unlike I used to tell my children, God does answer our *"Why"* questions.

Moments of sorrow are not meant to last a lifetime; the Bible clearly states these are times and seasons. You are not appointed to a miserable life, although there are a number of people that submit to just that. God has an appointed time and season for you to overcome the darkest moments that you experience.

And within every moment of sorrow, God makes Himself available to you. His word contains the answers that you need to heal; and to be whole. You are not to get stuck in the pain or memories of grief. God called you to continue on with your life.

In the Biblical sense, *sadness* is defined as bad, distress, wickedness, heavy grief, and evil. **None of these words describe God.** The problem with prolonged sadness or sorrow is that it weighs upon your mind. The more you meditate upon problems, heartache, sadness or death, the more you open yourself up to become a resting place or house for these types of things to live.

The only one that is happy with such a dreary scenario is Satan. That is because he wants to keep people in a sad and grieving state so that he can steal your dreams, kill your hopes and destroy your future.

That's not going to happen on my watch!

Like a hornet or a scorpion, Death has a sting. We can allow the spirit of God to comfort us with His Presence and truth so that sting will not infect our souls or affect your life like venom or poison affects the bloodstream. Satan is a thief and a liar.

The devil wants you to continually think about the mother, father, sister, brother, spouse, friend, child, or animal that you have lost; and become so overwhelmed with grief every time that you think about them that you feel as though you just can't go on living. If possible, he would like you to feel that same sadness over the loss of a job, money, reputation, status, lifestyle or any other thing that matters to you.

When you allow these feelings and emotions to have power over your life, you truly will not entertain thoughts about the joy or gladness that is available to you from the Lord. The devil's goal is to get you to **become so absorbed in your own grief** that you will over time destroy the important relationships that you still have. The objective is to put you into such emotional darkness that you will never be happy again.

But remember what you just read. Satan is a liar and a thief! You don't have to give him what he wants. In John 10:10, Jesus tells us that He came to ensure that we have abundant life. That word is a ray of *Son* Shine, warm and soothing to the soul.

Jesus did what He came to do, so abundant life is ours NOW!

You may ask, *"Are you saying that I should not even miss my mother, father, spouse, child, or friend?"*

No, that is not what is being stated here. What is being stated is that there is a difference between mourning the dead, missing someone that has died, and being overtaken by a spirit of grief.

To *mourn* a death is to express and exhibit the usual signs of sorrow common to most people. You will observe the behaviors customary to mourning, whether it is wearing black to a funeral or memorial, or gathering with family and friends to cry *and* laugh together. Regrets for lost opportunities, missed conversations and remembrances of shared good times are all a part of mourning.

Some cultures mourn by holding a wake; some host a send-off and raise a glass in a toast to celebrate a person's life. There are military honor guards and ceremonies that pay tribute to the memory of one who has served his or her country. These are examples of the various mourning traditions that people follow, and in a sense, it is a comfort to the mourners as they go through these customs.

In fact, Americans even have an annual Memorial Day with parades and ceremonies that pay honor to those that served their country. For certain the people that raise a glass to toast the dead find something to smile about before the night is over.

The absence of a loved one from the daily routine of living is also a familiar emotion. We miss the presence of people long after they have died. My own father, mother, brother, and more recently my sister have been dead for a number of years.

Growing up, I missed my father tremendously. I felt the sting of his absence from my life deep within my being. I still miss being able to talk with my mother. I even miss the lively disagreements and laughter I shared with my brother and sister.

Even today, I would love to have the chance to be able to sit down and have a conversation with my father. There is no longer an opportunity to build a relationship because he no longer lives in this earth. I miss my parents, my brother, sister, church members, and other relatives and friends that no longer live in the earth. I miss them, but I no longer grieve their loss.

I have too many wonderful memories and stories that I can tell about them that bring a smile to my face. *And, I can count my blessings for the wonderful family, peers, friends, and other people among the living that I still can create marvelous memories and stories with today.*

Did you know that the root word for "grieve" also translates into "grave"? To continually grieve over the death of someone is to carry the same pain, feel the same hurt and mental distress that you first felt years after the person has died. It can become a habit, and then a lifestyle.

You then live with a spirit of grief. It won't let you have joy or happiness. Instead it will wrap itself around you like a shroud. You were not designed to be wrapped up by the devil all the days of your life.

Think about that Hollywood version of the Grim Reaper with you cast into the role. That guy is just bad news roaming around seeing who he can siphon the life out of. Can you really see yourself carrying a scythe, walking around in a black hooded cloak looking forlorn and sorrow-full? There you walk, stripped to the bone with tears running down your skeletal face as you trudge valiantly from one place to another. Really?

Well, that's what the devil wants you to do.

Can you laugh at that picture? That's not you; you have much more sense than that. You are not a graveyard caricature; you are a joy giver. Your laughter is like a clap of thunder, a disturbance in the demonic realm. Remember, God made you to overflow with so much joy and laughter that you rout that ugly Grim Reaper right out of his place! Ha! Ha! Ha!

You know, in spite of all that has been said here, there are still some people that will violently defend and fight "to the death" for their right to continue grieving the demise of that loved one. They will say things like, "I will never get over this!" Reading these words, such an individual may feel defensive of his or her right to be sad about their loss; be it a person, a relationship or a dream.

They feel as though anyone who tries to minister joy to them is a threat or an enemy. It's as though they think that others do not understand what they are going through. No one else has experienced such a devastating loss. Nobody else knows what it is to love, or to lose someone, or to feel as though your heart or your gut has been ripped out of you. That's grief talking.

Now here is TRUTH.

God does understand. He cares about everything that you experience. That's why He gave you The Spirit of Joy. God designed you to be joyous, not to dwell in dark places in your mind. He designed your lips to curve upward in a smile, not down in a frown.

It is certainly understandable to miss the daily presence of our loved ones. But it needs to be a short season in which grief is allowed to have place. Let God wipe away your tears. Remember, you were designed to live in and walk in His Son Light. The lighter your soul, the freer and lighter you become.

Imagine that you are carrying two buckets, one on your right side, and the other on your left. These buckets are balanced on a beam that you are wearing across your shoulders. The beam that you are wearing is the yoke. One bucket has sorrow, doom and gloom; the other has peace, happiness and joy. Circumstances and events fill up the bucket of sorrow.

The peace, happiness and joy bucket is filled up with your choices and decisions to trust and believe God. The bucket of sorrow is not supposed to weigh you down. The only way that it can is if you don't choose to let God fill the other one.

There is sorrow in life, but we also have access to God's peace, happiness and joy. Jesus came to take the heavy burdens of life because He knows that we are not equipped to bear these burdens on our own.

He took the heavy burdens and left us balanced with His righteousness, peace, and joy. That's the Kingdom of God.

Actually, the scripture says that His yoke is easy and His burden is light. You don't have to feel guilty because you dwell among the living. You are free to live a good, happy life filled with joy and laughter. Isn't that good news!

Somebody cares so much about the quality of your life that He gave His own to ensure that you have peace, joy, happiness, light, laughter, goodness and abundance of blessing. He is the One who provides a remedy for the things that ail you. Isaiah 61 is very specific in showing us the kind of life God wants us to dwell in continually.

He gives us beauty for ashes, the oil of joy for mourning, and a garment of praise for a spirit of heaviness. He provides healing for the brokenhearted, comfort for all who mourn and He opens prison doors for those who are bound, whether by pain, sadness, grief or some other demonic chain.

Weep during the night, but then, get up in the morning and be infused with new life. You can sing for joy. You can shout, Glory Hallelujah! It's alright. God really does want you to **have a big grin, laugh out loud and be happy.**

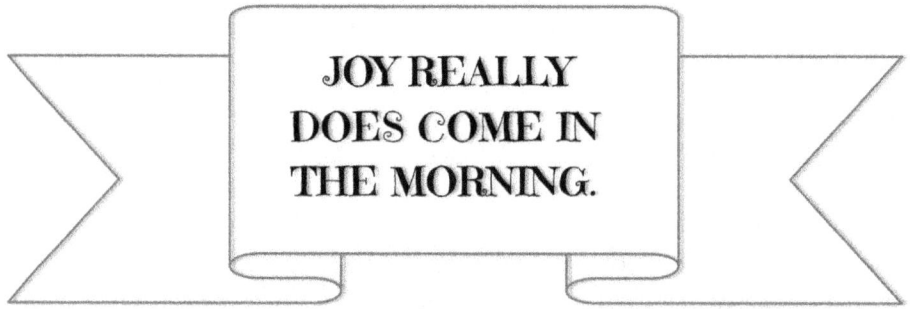

JOY REALLY DOES COME IN THE MORNING.

Your morning comes whenever you decide, "Morning is here!" Now that's something you can choose to *Smile, Laugh and Be Happy* about!

Scriptures: Psalm 116:15, 2Corinthians 5:8, Romans 12:15, Psalm 30:5, Romans 12:15, Psalm 30:5, Hebrews 13:5,

1Corinthians 15:55, John 10:10, Job 27:23, Isaiah 25:8b, Matthew 11:30

Happy Facts

Psalm 9:9 – *The Lord is my refuge and stronghold in times of trouble.*

Psalm 30:5 – *Weeping may endure for a night, but joy comes in the morning.*

Psalm 30:11 – *He turns my mourning into dancing and girds me with gladness.*

Psalm 46:1-3 – *God is my refuge in times of trouble.*

Psalm 46:10 – *When I am still, God lets me know that He can take care of all of me.*

Psalm 107:28-29 – *When I cry out to the Lord, He brings me out of distress, hushes the storm and stills the seas [of despair].*

Psalm 116:15 – *I know that the death of His saints is precious in the sight of God.*

Psalm 118:6 – *The Lord is on my side.*

Psalm 126:5 – *I may sow in tears, but I shall reap in joy and singing.*

Isaiah 25:8 – *Death is swallowed up in victory. God wipes away my tears.*

Isaiah 26:3 – *He keeps me in perfect peace.*

Isaiah 61:3 – *His spirit is upon me for consolation and joy.*

Jeremiah 15:16 – *His words are joy and rejoicing for my heart.*

Jeremiah 31:13 – *He turns my mourning into joy, as He comforts and makes me rejoice in Him.*

Nehemiah 8:10 – *His joy is my strength.*

John 14: 27 – *He gives me His peace, there is no need for my heart to be troubled.*

Romans 12:15 – *I rejoice with those who rejoice.*

Romans 15:13 – *The God of hope fills me with joy and peace so that I abound in hope.*

Philippians 4:6-7 – *In everything I give thanks. His peace guards my heart.*

Colossians 3:15 – *I let His peace rule in my heart.*

1Corinthians 15:26 – *Death is the final enemy, and it is defeated!*

1Peter 5:7 – *I can cast all of my cares upon Him, because God cares for me.*

My Happy Declarations

1. God cares about the quality of my life so much that He made provision for my joy even in the midst of sorrow. (Psalm 23)

2. I have a garment of praise that replaces the spirit of heaviness. (Isaiah 61:3)

3. I am anointed and overflow with God's joy and gladness. (Psalm 97:11, Isaiah 51:11)

4. My joyous laughter is a clap of thunder in the spirit realm. It sounds so loudly that it hisses the devil out of the places where I dwell. (Job 27:23)

5. God has turned my mourning into a dance of joy. (Psalm 30:11)

6. Jesus has succeeded in providing new, abundant life for me.

(John 10:10)

7. Morning is my opportunity to have a fresh new start.

8. I am strengthened with the joy of the Lord. (Zechariah 8:10)

9. No heavy burdens of sorrow for me. My bucket overflows with peace and joy!

Joy Keystones

I am passionately in love with God because He listens to me. He hears my prayers and answers them. As long as I live I'll keep praying to Him, for He stoops down to listen to my heart's cry. Death once stared me in the face, and I was close to slipping into its dark shadows. I was terrified and overcome with sorrow. I cried out to the Lord, "God, come and save me!" He was so kind, so gracious to me. Because of His passion toward me, He made everything right and He restored me. So I've learned from my experience that God protects the childlike and humble ones. For I was broken and brought low, but He answered me and came to my rescue! Now I can say to myself and to all, "Relax and rest, be confident and serene, for the Lord rewards fully those who simply trust in Him." God has rescued my soul from death's fear and dried my eyes of many tears. He's kept my feet firmly on His path and strengthened me so that I may please Him and live my life before Him in His life-giving light. Even when it seems I'm surrounded by many liars and my own fears, and though I'm hurting in my suffering and trauma, I still stay faithful to God and speak words of faith. So now, what can I ever give back to God to repay Him for the blessings He's poured out on me? I will lift up His cup of salvation and praise Him extravagantly for all that He's done for me. I will fulfill the promise I made to God in the presence of His gathered people. When one of God's holy lovers dies, it is costly to the Lord, touching His heart. Lord, because I am Your loving servant, You have broken open my life and freed me from my chains. Now I'll worship You passionately and bring to You my sacrifice of praise, drenched with thanksgiving! I'll keep my promise to You, God, in the presence of Your gathered people, just like I said I would. I will worship You here in Your living presence, in the temple in Jerusalem. I will worship and sing hallelujah, for I praise You, Lord! "

Psalm 116:1-19 TPT

HAPPY KEY #6

Laughter is an Anti-Aging Rx (Prescription)

"But those who wait on the Lord shall renew their strength; They shall mount up with wings like eagles; They shall run and not be weary, They shall walk and not faint." Isaiah 40:31

FIRST OF ALL, THERE IS NO SHAME in growing older. Truly you either die at a young age or live to a ripe old one. God has offered us 120 years if we will live for it, and the Bible says nothing about those years being despised.

This book continually emphasizes the importance of thinking happy thoughts because they really do help you to stay young at heart and renew your strength regardless of your chronological age. Consider this — even teenagers and young people can become old and tired when they refuse to think healthy thoughts.

Hooray, you made the right choice to let go of any thoughts of anger, revenge, unforgiveness, disappointment or regrets! You've begun to understand that it will stop your flow of the oil of joy and gladness.

That's why you are opting not to be dried up, brittle, or easily offended. You know that it would cause you more pain. I know that you will continue to move forward and live life this way. After all, you're still reading this book! This means that you are moving towards your fruitful and successful life.

Since you have chosen to guard your thoughts by going in a positive direction; go ahead and embrace the lovely, fresh, wholesome end of the spectrum of life. God wants you to have a lot of that. Keep on choosing the goodness of God for yourself.

Negativity is harsh on your spirit, soul and body, so don't allow it. It's debilitating, and ultimately creates sickness in your mind and physical body. Keep your ability to progress and process information correctly and have fruitful relationships. As you continue to cultivate faith, truth, joy and happiness you satisfy your stomach by the words of your mouth.

Good things grow within you, and a bright and cheery countenance settles upon you. Joy and happiness are an anti-aging prescription for life. The joy of the Lord is the true fountain of youth!

Laughing deep from the inside promotes health and well-being. Your heart registers a sense of cheerfulness, which transmits the message to your face – smile!

The more you smile, the greater your attraction to the people around you. You'll see the work was worth it as you enjoy healthy meaningful relationships and you begin to attract pleasant, encouraging people and experiences into your life. When you recognize that you're cultivating a better quality of life as you laugh; you will continue to speak and act accordingly.

Laughter is a true indication of faith in action, because it makes a bold statement of confidence and a happy heart. You are eliminating a habit of worry, because you know that God is taking care of everything that concerns you.

> *"A happy heart is good medicine and a cheerful mind works healing, but a broken spirit dries up the bones." Proverbs 17:22 AMPC*

Laughter brings moisture to your inward parts and releases the pent up emotions and pain that stem from cultivating resignation and disappointment in God. As you laugh, you release the endorphins that promote healing in your body.

> *"Let them shout for joy, and be glad, that favor my righteous cause: yea, let them say continually, Let the Lord be magnified, which hath pleasure in the prosperity of his servant." Psalm 35:27*

Go ahead, give a happy shout and let the laughter out. Remember, since you favor God's righteous cause, *you definitely have something to shout, Smile, Laugh and Be Happy about!*

Scriptures: Genesis 6:3, Proverbs 16:31, Isaiah 60:1, Proverbs 18:19, Philippians 4:6-8, Proverbs 15:16 AMPC, Proverbs 18:20-21, Psalm 138:8

Happy Facts

1. I celebrate every day and every birth year that I am on this earth.

2. I can grow older chronologically and maintain a youthful heart and mind. (Isaiah 40:31)

3. Thinking pure, lovely thoughts of good report refreshes my brain and brings peace to me. (Philippians 4:8)

4. Laughing energizes my inside and is God's special prescription for my continual good health. (Proverbs 17:22)

5. The more I smile, the more I attract the smiles of others. (Job 29:24 CEV)

6. The more things I laugh at, the more I eliminate worry from my life. (Matthew 6:25-33, 1 Thessalonians 5:16 AMPC)

My Happy Declarations

1. The more I smile and exhibit the joy of the Lord, the more I attract likeminded people, better experiences and better relationships toward myself. I am God's joy magnet!

2. My laughter is an indication of faith in action.

3. I laugh because I have complete confidence in God's plan for me.

4. I have full access to God's fountain of youth.

5. I have a happy heart.

Joy Keystones

"And my tongue shall talk of Your righteousness, rightness, and justice, and of [my reasons for] Your praise all the day long." Psalm 35:28 AMPC

"The light in the eyes [of him whose heart is joyful] rejoices the hearts of others, and good news nourishes the bones." Proverbs 15:30 AMPC

"Be happy [in your faith] and rejoice and be glad-hearted continually (always)..."
1 Thessalonians 5:16 AMPC

Something to think about...

Teeth are an interesting part of the human body. We do a lot of things with them.

Some people have pretty, even, naturally or dentally enhanced white ones (this includes dentures). Others have unattractive, deformed or stained yellow ones. Most people fall somewhere in between the bright and fright varieties.

We use our teeth to bite and chew, and we bare them when we are feeling joyful or angry. One of the best showcases for teeth is when we exhibit joy. Smiling and laughing rank among some of the best things in life that a person can do.

There is a lot of power within those moments of joyous expression. (Proverbs 17:22) Unfortunately, some of us are ashamed of the condition of our teeth, so we try to hide them from others. **Never be ashamed of your smile.** Don't be one of those people that only laugh with closed lips, and talk with your hand in front of your mouth. Be bold and exhibit the joy of the Lord.

Don't be one of those people that have perfectly acceptable teeth, but seldom smile because *"Life is too serious, there is never enough time for frivolity, and besides, what is there to laugh about?"* (Proverbs 15:13, Joel 2:21-27)

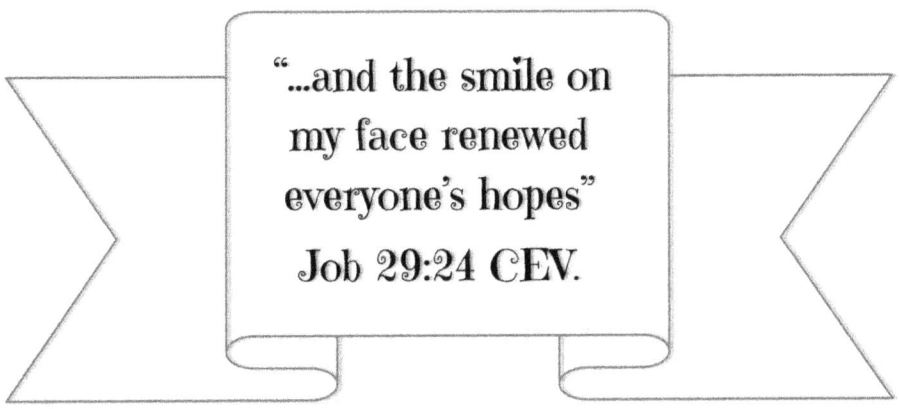

"...and the smile on my face renewed everyone's hopes" Job 29:24 CEV.

Remember, you are the light that shines in darkness; you are joy in the midst of sorrow. So, regardless of what you're working with: Floss, brush, whiten and SMILE! You're guaranteed to be a light to someone

Scriptures: Proverbs 17:22, Proverbs 15:13, Joel 2:21-27, Matthew 5:14, 16

.

A Joy Key From God's Word

There is no one in this earth that will ever be able to treat you better than God. Religion and tradition goes just so far and says, "He is able." But God says about Himself: "I will." I will bless you, I will deliver you, I will restore you, I will heal you, I will provide for you, I will protect you, I will give you peace and rest.

His "I will" is His will for your life being exercised and executed on your behalf. When you really think about it, it is astonishing how thoroughly the Father provides for His children. He has provided for every contingency, emergency, and sudden happenstance you could ever face, far in advance of your even experiencing it!

Did you know that after He triumphs over your enemies, the Lord rejoices over you with gladness and singing? His greatest joy and delight is found in His fearfully and wonderfully made creation.

He really is the Almighty God. He is your true Hero and Champion, the One that loves you with an everlasting love. He strengthens you on the inside, encourages, exhorts and trains you for victory, and He goes before you to ensure your victory in every challenge.

Say this aloud: "God really is rooting for me to succeed in my every endeavor. The Lord really does care about me. Jesus went to the cross so that I can live a joyous, abundant Kingdom life. I am the apple of God's eye; I'm engraved in the palms of His hands. He quiets my heart with His love, and He rejoices over me with singing. What a mighty God He is!"

Scriptures: Romans 8:31, Zephaniah 3:17, Psalm 139:15, Jeremiah 31:3, Ephesians 3:16, Psalm 144:1, Isaiah 45:2, 52:12,

Zechariah 2:8, Isaiah 49:16

Additional "I will" scriptures: Genesis 22:12, Exodus 3:12, Psalm 91:15 Matthew 8:3, Jeremiah 30:17, Joel 2:25 Romans 12:19, Matthew 4:19, Mark 1:17 Matthew 11:28, Luke 5:13, 21:15, John 6:40, 44 Acts 2:17, Romans 9:16, 2Corinthians 6:16

Today I Pray

Lord, I choose to smile, laugh and rejoice in Your everlasting goodness.

Thank You for reminding me that you delight in my prosperity and my joy. You quiet anxiety in my heart and rejoice over me with singing, so I sing happy songs in honor of You.

I delight in the knowledge that I belong to You. I am grateful for Your continual involvement in everything that concerns me. I am humbled at the recognition that You care so much about every aspect of my life. You strengthen me with your joy even as you deliver me from my enemies.

I desire to know you as the Lord of my happiness, for truly You alone can fill my heart with joy. Thank You, Father for Your tender mercies and loving kindness towards me.

You give me a genuine reason to smile, sing and shout, for You are good, and Your goodness and mercy endures forever! Thank You, Lord, for the blessings that You have made just for this day. Today I rejoice and am glad. In Jesus' Name, Amen.

Scriptures: Zephaniah 3:17, Nehemiah 8:10, Psalm 138:8, Psalm 18:48, Psalm 25:6, 145:9, 1Chronicles 16:41, Psalm 136, Psalm 118:24

IT'S TIME TO CELEBRATE AND GIVE PRAISE TO THE LORD!

HEART OF JOY SONG

Words by Lonzine Lee
Can be sung to the tune of "Bingo"

I have a heart that's filled with joy
And Jesus is the reason!
He's so good to me,
My heart is filled with joy.
My heart is filled with joy,
And Jesus is the reason!

This joy I have, it overflows
And Jesus is the reason!
He's so good to me,
My joy overflows.
My joy overflows
And Jesus is the reason!

When I laugh, joy heals my soul
And Jesus is the reason!
He's so good to me,

Laughter heals my soul.
Laughter heals my soul
And Jesus is the reason!

He's so ... [*good to me*]
He's so ... [*good to me*]
My heart is filled with joy
And Jesus is the reason!

HAPPY KEY #7

Kindness is A Law of Mercy

"Therefore, as the elect of God, holy and beloved, put on tender mercies, kindness, humility, meekness, longsuffering; 13bearing with one another, and forgiving one another, if anyone has a complaint against another; even as Christ forgave you, so you also must do." Colossians 3:12-14

DOESN'T YOUR HEART REJOICE WHEN you realize you are forgiven? It is liberating to actually know that you have been released from the weight of guilt and sin. The goodness and kindness of God is extended to you. It is available to you in every area of your life, including your thoughts and actions. All you have to know is:

"...that if you confess with your mouth the Lord Jesus and believe in your heart that God has raised Him from the dead, you will be saved. For with the heart one believes unto righteousness, and with the mouth confession is made unto salvation." Romans 10:9-1

Confess the Lordship of Jesus with your mouth (that means

ownership, giving up your rights and accepting Him as total Possessor); believe it in your heart. That is our induction into accepting God's mercy and forgiveness; receiving the salvation and sonship He provided through The Lord Jesus Christ.

A most excellent part is exploring the rights, privileges and responsibilities that you just inherited. Once you have received His liberty for yourself, it allows you to find out about the endless bounties you have just acquired.

Once you have found out about the blessings and responsibilities of your Kingdom citizenship, you can and are even expected to extend the same opportunity to others. You are commanded to forgive those who offend, hurt or speak against you in order to promote the flow of forgiveness in your life and develop the precious fruit of the Spirit.

This is the very fruit that works in you to bring health, wealth and success in every aspect of your life.

Love, joy, peace, patience, kindness, goodness, faithfulness, gentleness and self-control are strong allies that empower you to prosper in everything. They are also powerful weapons to have in your spiritual arsenal.

Practicing random and sometimes on purpose acts of kindness is a popular cultural trend in secular society.

IN GOD'S KINGDOM, KINDNESS IS NOT A RANDOM ACT; IT IS A FRUIT OF THE SPIRIT.

Our Father would rather that you actually *become kind* by incorporating the fruit of kindness into your daily living. Extending true kindness and forgiveness takes courage. You have it in you to be kind; but you have to activate it. In fact, kindness is a spiritual law; however it is your choice to allow it to flow out of you.

You have the power to increase the flow of joy, hope and happiness in this earth. Every day of your life you have the opportunity to release kindness, compassion, consideration and forgiveness into the lives of the people around you. Think about how soothing it is to your soul when you receive an encouraging word from someone. How great does it feel when you provide an encouraging word for someone else? Wow!

You have the power to positively affect another person's life. Now that's a happy thought, *and a reason to Smile, Laugh and Be Happy!*

Scriptures: Matthew 6:9, Ephesians 4:32, Galatians 5:22-24, Proverbs 31:26

Happy Facts

1. The Word of the Lord is my joy. (Jeremiah 15:16)
2. The joy of the Lord is my strength. (Nehemiah 8:10)
3. I am strong and maturing in the joy of the Lord. (Psalm 21:1)
4. Kindness is a spiritual law of mercy in my heart and comes out of my mouth. (Proverbs 31:26)
5. Looking for opportunities to be kind to others every chance I get is powerful. It is not just words, but an expression of God's Word in action. (Galatians 6:10)
6. I have the faith to be kind and extend forgiveness toward others just as Christ has shown kindness to me. (Ephesians 4:32)
7. Compassion, mercy and kindness are all spiritual fruit, and like joy they flow from inside of me. (Ephesians 5:9 AMP)
8. Being kind is the will of God for me. (Ephesians 4:32)

My Happy Declaration

When I extend forgiveness, kindness and consideration toward the people around me, I increase the flow of joy, hope and happiness into this earth and within myself.

Joy Keystones

"²² The Holy Spirit produces a different kind of fruit: *unconditional* love, joy, peace, patience, kindheartedness, goodness, faithfulness, ²³ gentleness, and self-control. You won't find any law opposed to fruit like this. ²⁴ Those of us who belong to the Anointed One have crucified our old lives and put to death the flesh and all the lusts and desires that plague us.
²⁵ *Now* since we have chosen to walk with the Spirit, let's keep each step in perfect sync with God's Spirit. ²⁶ This will happen when we set aside our self-interests *and work together to create true community* instead of a culture consumed by provocation, *pride,* and envy."

Galatians 5:22-26 VOICE

HAPPY KEY #8

Gentleness is a Power Source

"Brethren, if a man is overtaken in any trespass, you who are spiritual restore such a one in a spirit of gentleness, considering yourself lest you also be tempted. 2Bear one another's burdens, and so fulfill the law of Christ." Galatians 6:1-2

G ENTLENESS FLOWS OUT OF A patient, grateful and generous heart. A generous person has a willing, obedient heart that is yielded to God's will. Gentle people look for the best in people, patiently filtering the heartfelt cry of the soul regardless of the tone of voice. They look beyond the exterior facial expression to see the heart of the matter.

You have the ability in you, so choose to be that which you are. Be that gentle person because The Holy Spirit is in you.

I thought about this as I was reading about Betsie ten Boom in the book, *The Hiding Place* by her sister, Corrie ten Boom. Even as a prisoner in a Nazi concentration camp, Betsie expressed that gentle, wise, and powerful heart of God. You and I possess it also. We must humble ourselves to release that gentle power of love in order for real power to become evident in our lives.

Gentle people are strong, not weaklings or pushovers; they are powerful individuals that walk in gratitude, humility and meekness before the Lord. It is impossible to take advantage of or dominate a truly gentle, humble person. They seek to maintain unity of the Spirit and peace in their atmosphere, and they obey God's commands in order to see it manifest. Gentle people do not compromise the word of the Lord.

They will agree quickly with adversaries, but they will not bow to intimidation or oppression. They know how to choose their battles, and they choose to fight on the winning side. They understand that the greater One lives in them, and that the attitudes that are pleasing in the world are surpassed by the attitude of gratitude and obedience that pleases God. Pleasing God is all that matters to them.

You really are master over your mind and emotions. You just need to believe and execute God's word on the subject. If you want to be pleasing to God, obey what He says. Believe that He rewards those who truly believe enough to seek Him in order to obey. If you follow what is said in His word, it's easy to be patient, gentle, and kind to others and live this way on a daily basis. Now your flesh may not think that it's easy, but your spirit will remind you that it is always easier to choose God's way.

It takes a redeemed, humble, loving and generous heart to overlook derision and scorn from hurting souls. Gentle people walk in that kind of humility. They do not create mental lists of perceived offenses from other people. Instead, they walk in love, taking no account of wrong done toward them.

They have already decided to forgive and pray for the people and situation because they do not take personal offense. They see the other person as the one who is hurting and in need of prayer. You and I have the capacity for that kind of generosity.

I can just hear you saying, *"Lord give me patience. Increase my faith."*

"By your patience possess your souls." Luke 21:19

We are instructed to rule over our own spirits. You and I have the capacity for discipline, patience and temperance in all things. We just don't always have the desire to exercise this capacity. Master your emotions; you are not enslaved or indebted to your flesh.

Possess your soul! If you don't master it, it leaves you exposed to attacks that you may not easily overcome. Stand your ground and develop integrity and a strong commitment to the cause and people of God.

You've already learned the power of cultivating kindness and forgiveness, so you know that this is really the way that you were created to be. As you put these principles into effect, you will reap the Kingdom benefits and grow deeper in love with God and God's creation. Are you ready? Can't you just see yourself walking in the power of gentleness and love? I hope your answer is, "Yes."

As you allow the love of God to flow from and through you to others, they will recognize that you are one of God's true disciples.

Now that is a *Smile, Laugh and Be Happy* thought!

Scriptures: Ephesians 4:2-3, Matthew 5:25, 1John 4:4, Hebrews 11:6, Proverbs 16:7, 2Corinthians 7:32, Proverbs 25:28, 1Corinthians 13:4-8, Romans 8:2, John 13:34-35

Happy Facts

1. I am equipped to be a gentle, humble person because Holy Spirit is active within me. (2 Timothy 2:24-26)

2. I have an obedient and willing heart that is yielded to the will of God. (Isaiah 1:19)

3. I am gentle, which means that I am not weak, but powerful in humility and meekness in the sight of God. (Psalm 37:11, Joel 3:10)

4. I seek to maintain unity of the Spirit in the bond of peace. (Ephesians 4:2-3)

5. Because the greater One lives in me, I have overcome the power that would please the ungodliness of my flesh. (1 John 4:4)

6. I agree quickly with my adversaries. I don't have to appear to be "right" in the sight of others. (Matthew 5:25)

7. I am master over my own emotions, not the slave of my feelings. (1 Corinthians 9:25, Romans 8:2-14, Proverbs 25:28)

8. I have the capacity for the Kingdom (God) kind of generosity. (Proverbs 16:32, Matthew 20:14-15, 1 Corinthians 4:20-21)

My Happy Declarations

1. It is my choice to look beyond the frowning faces and

haughty demeanors that others may direct toward me. (Jeremiah 1:17-19, James 5:20)

2. I choose to cultivate a willing and obedient heart, and walk in God's generosity of spirit toward the people in my midst. (Isaiah 1:19, 1 Peter 4:8)

3. I am one of His vessels of love, joy, peace, gentleness and restoration in this earth! (2 Corinthians 13:11, Galatians 5:22)

Joy Keystone

"My spiritual brothers and sisters, if one *of our faithful* has fallen into a trap and is snared by sin, *don't stand idle and watch his demise.* Gently restore him, being careful not to step into your own snare. ² Shoulder each other's burdens, and then you will live as the law of the Anointed teaches us. ³ Don't *take this opportunity to* think you are better than those who slip because you aren't; then you *become the fool and* deceive even yourself. ⁴ Examine your own works so that if you are proud, it will be because of your own accomplishments and not someone else's. ⁵ Each person has his or her own burden to bear *and story to write.*"

Galatians 6:1-5 VOICE

Happy Song Joy Exercise...

By Lonzine Lee

Here's a fun little happy song joy exercise for you. Instead of using a familiar melody, you begin by speaking the laugh syllables on each line aloud in a 1-2-3-4 beat, one beat for each syllable. Here's a practice count: 1-2-3-4 = Ha-ha, Ha-ha.

The count will change as you get toward the end (1-2-3 = Te-he-he). You got it? It's okay if you don't. Once you get into a rhythm, you'll be fine. It's just for fun, no one will even know if you get off beat. But you will seem a bit silly.:) Are you ready? Great, let's begin.

Ha-ha, Ha-ha
Ho-ho, Ho-ho
He-he, He-he
Woo-hoo, Woo-hoo

Ha-ha, Ha-ha
Ho-ho, Ho-ho
He-he, He-he
Woo-hoo, Woo-hoo

Ha-ha, Ha-ha, Ha-ha, Ha-ha
Ho-ho, Ho-ho, Ho-ho, Ho-ho
He-he, He-he, He-he, He-he
Woo-hoo, Woo-hoo, Woo-hoo

Hoo!

Te-he-he, Woo-woo-hoo *(1-2-3, 1-2-3 count)*
Ha-ha-ha, Ho-ho-hoo *(1-2-3, 1-2-3 count)*

Te-he, Ha-ha, Ho-ho

Woo

Te-he, Ha-ha, Ho-ho

Woo

Now, if you spoke the words, all the way through,
We actually got a laugh out of you!

Woo hoo! Congratulations. You just took a moment to *Smile, Laugh and Be Happy!*

HAPPY KEY #9

Peace Manifests Through Forgiveness

"And let the peace of God rule in your hearts, to which also you were called in one body; and be thankful." Colossians 3:15

YOU ARE A HAPPY PERSON when you allow the peace of God to permeate you and flow out of your inner being through words, actions and songs that minister to others. You are a happier and healthier person when you forgive and release others from judgment and extend mercy toward those who have wronged you. Once you've forgiven others, you get to enjoy the peace of God.

God Himself planted His peace into your heart through His Holy Spirit. It's interesting how God equates receiving His peace with releasing forgiveness to others. If you want peace, you have to sacrifice pride and other negative emotions, and allow His forgiveness and love to flow into you. Forgiving others unlocks the door to peace, because as you forgive others, God forgives you.

Your life is not meant to be ruled by your opinion or

emotions. God's peace is meant to rule your heart. Just as forgiveness flows into you, it is also meant to flow out of you toward others. But first, you receive it for yourself. Once God's forgiveness fills your heart, you are empowered to allow His peace to rule in place of negative thoughts, feelings and emotions. You learn how to love others on God's terms.

His peace provides comfort, instruction and rest. In order to live in God's peace, you simply obey God and choose to allow it to reign in your heart. An unforgiving spirit causes stress to the whole man – he or she is out of alignment with the will of God. The peace of God de-stresses your soul and your physical body. In fact it promotes wellness and life for all who choose to cultivate the discipline and strength of obedience that derives from pursuing it.

Receiving and obeying God's correction, being malleable even when it goes against feelings and familiar behavior chastens us, which yields the peaceable fruit of righteousness. Chastening builds character and develops discipline, which is what empowers and strengthens you from the inside out. Why is this discipline so important? It is important because in order to pursue and obtain peace, you have to first depend upon God Himself. Simply put, this is the action of seeking and esteeming your relationship with God and His Kingdom above any other desire.

Which one do you desire to contain on a consistent basis; the happiness, joy, faith, freedom and restfulness that comes from the peace of God or the twisted, depressing, doubt-filled, soul-destroying stress of unforgiveness? You can't contain both within your body; you can't live with double standards. You can only have one or the other, God's peace or stress and anxiety.

Of course you are wise to choose peace. Imagine someone saying, "Ooh, ooh, I want to be twisted, depressed and stressed.

I just can't forget what they did, I just can't forgive. I'd prefer to continue to destroy my soul daily. I would rather get wrinkly and ugly and hold on to unforgiveness while the other brother goes on living life. I'll just dry up like a raisin, blame everyone else for my problems and feel sorry for myself because God won't just change for me."

Well, someone might actually feel and say something like that. But that someone is not you. Ha Ha! You've been paying attention. You know that as you are quick to hear and slow to anger, you will find yourself both willing and ready to forgive others their faults.

Peace just feels too good to allow yourself to be bothered with negativity. Freedom and joy are just too refreshing to take up or hold onto the staleness of yesterday's offenses any longer. Your heart is singing,

"I embrace this peaceful life. God is too good, life is too sweet, and life is just too glad to go back to the bad! Good-bye ugly days, good-bye!"

In other words, the Good said, "bye-bye" to that ugly and revengeful life of the past.

God's peace is more than a calm or tranquil atmosphere. Peace is wholeness, there is nothing missing. It is everything you need. It manifests in the middle of or the absence of pain, anger, bitterness, judgments, or any kind of an unforgiving heart. In exchange you have a spirit of reconciliation. You don't have to maintain a dark cloud in your mind anytime you look at certain people.

Peace rescues you from the derangement of mental torment that exists in the minds of restless, resentful, bitter people. God keeps you in perfect peace as you keep your mind fixed on His goodness. This is pleasing to Him. Let it also be pleasing to you.

The peace of God really does surpass all human capacity for understanding. It is the perfect protector, guarding our hearts and minds from all the threats to our well-being. Peace protects your thought life. The Amplified Bible says that it transcends all understanding even as it garrisons [builds a fort] and mounts guard over our hearts. While you may not know how to describe His peace, rest assured you will recognize it when it comes. Yahoo!

A person of peace disperses joy into the atmosphere and provides a safe haven for a wounded or troubled person, because his or her life is full of God's peace. It is the will of the Lord that you speak peace in uncertain or tumultuous situations and times.

You are in this earth to promote The Kingdom of God's wisdom, harmony and well-being. You are one of God's peacemakers, a promoter of love, health, wealth and wisdom.

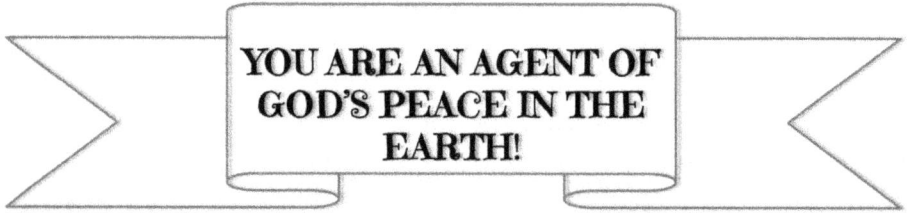

YOU ARE AN AGENT OF GOD'S PEACE IN THE EARTH!

Rejoice! Yahoo! That's a powerful reason to *Smile, Laugh, and Be Happy!*

Scriptures: Colossians 3:16-67, Matthew 6:14-15, Mark 11:25, Hebrews 12:11-14, Proverbs 4:20-22 AMPC, James 3:16-18, Matthew 6:33, James 1:19, Isaiah 26:3, Hebrews 12:15, Philippians 4:708, Mark 4:39

Happy Facts

1. I cultivate the discipline of obeying the word of God in order to yield the peaceable fruit of righteousness in me. (Hebrews 12:11)

2. God's peace protects my mind. (Philippians 4:7)

3. I am a God-ordained peacemaker. (James 3:18)

4. I diffuse joy into the atmosphere, which will affect troubled and wounded people for the good. (Romans 5:3, 15:13)

5. I am both willing and prompt to extend forgiveness toward others. (Ephesians 4:32)

6. I am an agent of God's peace in the earth. (Luke 10:5-6

7. I am in this earth to promote the Kingdom of God's wisdom, unity and happiness. (James 3:18)

8. God's peace is planted in my heart through His Word. All of my needs are met because of His peace. (Acts 10:36, Philippians 4:7)

My Happy Declarations

1. I'm a peacemaker; I seek to forgive others quickly so that I can maintain this good and perfect gift from above.

2. God's peace just feels too good to allow myself to be bothered with negativity and unforgiveness.

3. Peace is rooted in my relationship with God Himself.

4. Because of my faith in Jesus, I have peace with God. (Romans 5:1)

Joy Keystones

"Be kind to one another, tenderhearted, forgiving one another, even as God in Christ forgave you."
Ephesians 4:32

"Since we have been *acquitted and* made right through faith, we are able to experience *true and lasting* peace with God through our Lord Jesus, the Anointed One, *the Liberating King.*"
Romans 5:1 VOICE

Something To Think About...

Have you ever looked at the traits of happy people? If you have, you can't help but notice that happy people receive what they want out of life. It's because they know how to be grateful. They choose to bypass the many opportunities for expressing dissatisfaction, offense and complaints, and they focus on the good or positive side of things. (Read this again, this is good)

Happy people are not brainless individuals that go around with a saccharine, "I'm happy, happy, happy!" demeanor or sappy smile on their faces. They just allow less negativity into their brains than other people. When you let nothing offend you, you naturally move forward.

Happy, joyful people are not jealous, sad or miserable. Joyful people will have doors opened for them. Depression cannot overtake a joyful person. Happy people bring joy and gladness to the people around them; consequently, people are [dare I say it] happy to have them around.

Happy and joyful thoughts are detoxes for negativity, and a tonic for good health. Remember Proverbs 17:22, "...a merry heart does good like a medicine."

So go ahead and T-H-I-N-K yourself healthy and happy!

A Joy Key About God, His Word And You

Do you want to do, have, and be more than you have ever been for yourself and others? If your answer is yes, the Bible has the answers to how you can have what you want. It provides instructions for daily living, getting along with different kinds of people, handling finances, and decision-making.

The Word of God teaches you how to hear the voice of the Lord, raise your children, prosper in all of your relationships, and it even provides resources for education. But the answers don't just pop out of the pages. We have to read and study it.

The Bible does not come right out and say move to California, put on a blue shirt, eat yogurt for breakfast or invite the new couple at church over for dinner. But it does teach you how to listen for and hear the voice of God for yourself.

It teaches you about His character so that you recognize His blessings upon the good things in life. The Bible also provides you with the essential principles you need to make wise and informed choices, maintain your body as the temple of Holy Spirit, and show yourself friendly to others.

The governments, kingdoms and people of the secular world may be experiencing rough economical and emotional times. There are also a number of Christian people that choose to live defeated lives and experience misery, just like the inhabitants of the world. However, there is an essential difference between the two groups – one has a Biblical and the other has a humanistic solution.

The worldly kingdom lives independent of God's assistance or leadership. The people of this world place their hope in their own or someone else's ability to provide solutions or fix their problems. But no matter how many turn-key solutions, government programs or false religion doctrines they devise, they all turn out to be short-lived.

Despite the best possible human efforts, humanity does not have the ability to successfully defeat Satan or survive in this earth without the intervention and help of God.

On the other wise, citizens of God's Kingdom, even if they currently live a defeated lifestyle, have access to provision and relief in Jesus Christ. We can choose to be delivered anytime we accept and activate our repentance, faith and obedience. Through Jesus we have stability in our times and access to Father God's wisdom and knowledge.

Jesus did not leave us alone in this world. We have an Advocate and a Helper who is God in the Person of Holy Spirit. He was sent into the world specifically to lead and guide us in our Kingdom lives. He teaches us how to use our God-given authority to live in continual victory in this earth with Heaven's power.

You have access to the true Hope that is needed to avoid fear, anxiety and an underlying sense of despair. You are a fountain of God's wisdom, love and knowledge in this earth.

The joy key here is that you have nothing to fear. You can be glad and rejoice because the Lord will do marvelous things through you. You are a vital part of His good news package for the world.

He downloads solutions into your heart and brain so that you can act upon them for yourself and relay them to others. Remember, He wants to empower you to get wealth so that He can bless other people, even nations through you

Do you realize that the execution of one original idea from God is enough to transform the lives of a multitude? He wants to give you creative solutions to the problems that you face in life. If you will trust and obey His instructions, not only will your life improve, but you will positively affect improvement in the lives of others as well. **You were created to be a resource** for the people of this world. That's really something to get excited about.

This is your time to expect an original idea from the Lord that will give you seed to sow. In other words, you can expect to get something from Him that enables you to bless yourself and others. Okay, it's true that you may not get the solution to instantly relieve all the world's hunger problems. But you can get direction on how to help feed people in need within your community. Get excited, this is your time to hear from Him and advance the Kingdom all over the world. Rejoice, and be a key to solving a problem for someone else. That's where it starts.

Now that you know that God wants to bless you, you can learn how to expect a financial harvest and financial relief for your household, your church and those around you. So expect it. Obey His commands to rejoice and speak His word, and receive His instructions that lead to manifested provision. And remember, when you get it, share it with others and you will have more coming.

God wants to talk to you! You don't have to have a college education, formal business training or a full ordination to hear from Him. If you faithfully seek Him with the intention to listen for His answer and obey His instructions, you will get His wisdom and knowledge with understanding.

You will not be disappointed. You will be a blessing to the people around you as you direct others to the Deliverer and Lord, Jesus Christ. Isn't this exciting! You can tell your neighbors that there is no need to fear; there is stability in these days and the strength of salvation is seen, because *you have chosen to be a vessel of God's love, wisdom and knowledge.*

Glory to God, it's time to clap your hands, sing, laugh, be glad, shout and dance, because the Lord is doing marvelous things for and through you!

Scriptures: Psalm 20:7, John 14:16, 26; 15:5, Isaiah 33:6, Romans 5:2, Ephesians 2:18, 3:12; Joel 2:21, Galatians 3:8, Deuteronomy 8:7-18, Isaiah 45:11, 1John 2:1, 14:16, Luke 6:38, 1Peter 2:6

Joy In The Truth Of His Word

"Wisdom and knowledge will be the stability of your times, and the strength of salvation; the fear of the Lord is His treasure." Isaiah 33:6

"Fear not, O land; be glad and rejoice: for the LORD will do great things." Joel 2:21

"...that the God of our Lord Jesus Christ, the Father of glory, may give to you the spirit of wisdom and revelation in the knowledge of Him, the eyes of your understanding being enlightened; that you may know what is the hope of His calling, what are the riches of the glory of His inheritance in the saints and what is the exceeding greatness of His power toward us who believe, according to the working of His mighty power..." Ephesians 1:17-19

"Let your character or moral disposition be free from love of money [including greed, avarice, lust, and craving for earthly possessions] and be satisfied with your present [circumstances and with what you have]; for He [God] Himself has said, I will not in any way fail you nor give you up nor leave you without support. [I will] not, [I will] not, [I will] not in any degree leave you helpless nor forsake nor let [you] down (relax My hold on you)! [Assuredly not!] So we take comfort and are encouraged and confidently and boldly say, The Lord is my Helper; I will not be seized with alarm [I will not fear or dread or be terrified]. What can man do to me?" Hebrews 13:5-6 AMPC

Today I Pray...

I bless You Lord with all of my soul and everything that is within me. I will not forget all of your benefits, for truly You have blessed me. Because of You, I am blessed with the ability to choose love, joy and happiness on a daily basis. You have lightened my soul and graced me with the ability to overcome darkness in my thoughts, words and actions. I give You praise and thanks for granting me a happy heart.

I know that you are not what Christians and others have portrayed you as, a dour or sour Sovereign. You are not that mean Deity sitting on a throne waiting for the opportunity to ruin lives or destroy hopes. Thank you, Father, You are the giver of hope, the fulfiller of dreams, and the Source of true joy, happiness, peace, health, and wholeness. I'm so glad that I belong to You. I'm so glad to be a part of Your Kingdom, and a partaker of Your grace. As I am learning to walk in your joy and happiness, You even grant me the ability to be and live well.

Lord, I want my life to reflect Your goodness and mercy. I want the people around me to see how blessed and wise it is to live a life inhabited by your Presence. I want to be a showcase, a displayer of Your Divine blessing, living proof that anyone who really chooses to be inhabited by You will never regret it. This life with you is so, so exciting and inviting if I were not already in it I would definitely dive in immediately.

Out of my belly and mouth flow Your words of love, exhortation, edification and encouragement. When I speak, I do so as the oracles of God. I choose to smile, laugh aloud, and sing for the joy of belonging to You. I have to rejoice, because You just fill me up with gladness! It is just so good to sing and give praises to Your name!

This is the day that You have made. Your faithfulness is great towards me. It is a new opportunity for me to be glad and rejoice in You and the new mercies of the day. This is the day in which I become known to all I come in contact with as a carrier of the joy of the Lord. I am Your obedient vessel, I am changed for the better by Your Word.

I am redeemed and I say so, because now I know that You want me to be happy. You like blessing me because You want me to be blessed. You want me to overflow with Your joy. My cup overflows with Your blessing. Oh, what a wonderful God and Father You are to us all! I am so glad in You that I just have to shout: THANK YOU LORD! THANK YOU, THANK YOU, THANK YOU! Truly You are good to me. Amen.

Scripture References: Psalm 16:5-9, 23:5-6, 24:8, 92:1-5, 103:1, 107:2, 118:24;
Lamentations 3:22-23, Colossians 3:16, Hebrews 3:13, 1Peter 4:11, 2Corinthians 1:4, 8:1, Ephesians 4:29

> **IT'S TIME TO CELEBRATE AND GIVE PRAISE TO THE LORD!**

THE PRAISE FOR YOUR GOODNESS SONG

Words by Lonzine Lee
Can be sung to the tune of "Yankee Doodle"

When I start to praise You, Lord
My heart begins to open,
It makes me happy just to know
Your power can't be broken.

You, O Lord blessed me with joy,
Through You I am forgiven,
Your love is patient – it is kind,
I thank You for your goodness.

Lord, You are so good to me
I just can't keep from smiling
I want all of my friends to know
That You are my Provider.

You're my Savior and my Friend,
You are my Deliverer.
You're the Source of all my peace
I praise You for your goodness!

I praise You for your goodness!
I praise You for your goodness!

Happy Key #10

Love and Obedience: Keys to the Fear of the Lord

"But earnestly desire and zealously cultivate the greatest and best gifts and graces (the higher gifts and the choicest graces). And yet I will show you a still more excellent way [one that is better by far and the highest of them all — love]" 1 Corinthians 12:31 AMPC

THE FEAR OF THE LORD is the beginning of wisdom and knowledge. The lack of the fear of the Lord is how fools live. You should already be smiling as you read these words. Why? Because the greatest key that you have is the love of God. In fact, Love and Obedience are the two sides of the Master Key.

The Love of God overcomes every obstacle and silences every argument. This is the power that never fails, never gives up, never goes out of style and is always available. The well-kept secret is that this world needs to be provoked and injected with the love of God inside of you. In other words, His love needs to be manifesting through you daily in your home, play, work, every place that you go.

You are a vessel of God's Astounding Love. It is in your heart, ready to flow out of your life and then your mouth. It is anchored by hope that does not disappoint. Think about that. The love that you have inside of you never disappoints, it is only capable of succeeding and exceeding expectations. God's love exceeds your ability to comprehend its generosity and goodness. This is the love that you have inside of you! As His Kingdom representative, you re-present His love in this world.

Whether acknowledged or not, God's love [which is His word and power] sustains and holds everything and everyone together. If His love were not present and available to be expressed through His sons, the whole world would be overshadowed by evil. However, God's love is the shining light in this earth and we are the children of that Light. God's light is always able to dispel the works of darkness in your life.

All who are in Christ are commanded to live the life and walk in love, because God is the living, vibrating love inside you. You have the frequency and capacity available to you to give and receive God's great love. You are love-wired and have what it takes to love the seemingly unlovely, starting with yourself and then other people.

You have what it takes to cease being so unlovely yourself. God perfects the things in this earth through His love. He works through us, His sons, as vessels to pour His everlasting love through. Why? To reach the precious ones that live as orphans - lost, hurting, and dying people of this world.

Those who are not in Christ do not know the true love story of God and His creation. God's love is giving; it fills and changes lives for the better. His love is pure, generous and clean instead of being selfish, lustful or pride filled. It is rooted in Jesus' unselfish gift of His own life in order to save the many.

What a contrast to the "What's in it for me?" mentality so prevalent in the world today. You can walk free from the fears of the world when you walk in the fear and love of God. You have a covenant of protection, and a Name to call upon whenever you need Him.

Jesus honored His Father and walked in the obedient spirit of the fear of the Lord. He did not fear mankind, the world or the devil. He feared and reverenced His Father. You don't have to fear failure, circumstances or the opinions of others. Walk in obedience to God's commands, and you are living and moving in the Spirit of the Fear of the Lord. You are walking in honor and reverence of God. According to the Bible, this is the love of God.

Rejoice that you please the Lord when you choose to care more about what He thinks and desires of you than you do about the opinions and demands of your fleshly desires and the criticism from others. He wants to pour His goodness into you and flow it through you into the lives of the very people that speak against you. He desires to bless you and free you from any and everything that would try to destroy you. He has been giving of Himself to you since before you were ever born.

To love God means walking in the fear of the Lord by obeying His statutes and His commands. You will enjoy it more and more as you do it a little more every day. Know from your inside that as you are willing and obedient to love God and walk in the fear of the Lord, you will succeed. Remember, Jesus learned obedience on a daily basis, by choosing His Father's will in everything.

> *"Though He were a Son, yet learned He obedience by the things which He suffered; And being made perfect, He became the author of eternal salvation*

unto all them that obey Him..." Hebrews 5:8-9

As you go and likewise choose the Father's will in everything, you will achieve spectacular results working with Him. He's in you to help you overcome every battle and succeed in every endeavor that you trust Him to lead you through. Remember our foundation key; God is on your side. He's for you, not against you. He made you to be more than a conqueror. You can do this!

You can be more in this earth than you ever thought you would be. You can be successful in areas where you or others have doubted your abilities. You're not alone; you have help from the Most High God. Remember, He is the greater One. No one can defeat Him, and He lives in you!

Rejoice and be glad, God in you is your hope of glory. Shout out loud, you have a reason to be glad! This world is filled with sad people who need the gladness that God has equipped you to give. Love never fails, so He won't fail as He works in and through you. If He won't fail, you won't fail. And if you fall, He will pick you up as you obey Him. That's a guarantee. Expect it. Live for Him.

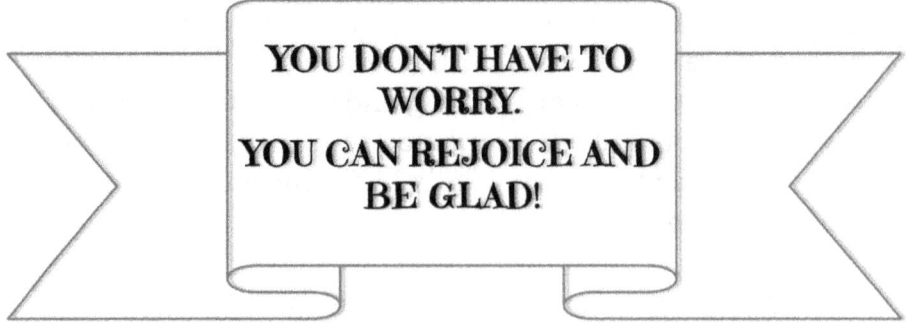

YOU DON'T HAVE TO WORRY.
YOU CAN REJOICE AND BE GLAD!

Now you know that you have something to *Smile, Laugh and Be Happy* about.

Scriptures: Psalm 111:10, Proverbs 1:7, 1Corinthians 13, Romans 5:5, Ephesians 3:20, 1John 4:17, 2Corinthians 4:6, 1Thessalonians 5:5, Romans 12:21, Hebrews 1:3, John 15:13-14, 1John 4:12, John 3:16, 1Timothy 2:5-6, 1John 3:16, Psalm 91, Philippians 2:9-10, 1John 5:2-3, 2John 1:6, 1John 4:18, Matthew 16:23-26, Hebrews 11:6, 13:6 Jeremiah 1:15, John 3:16, 1 Timothy 2:3-6 Isaiah 1:19 Daniel 11:32b, Romans 8:31, 37, 1 John 4:4 Colossians 1:7, 1Corinthians 13:4-8

Happy Facts

1. The love of God and my obedience are my greatest keys to happiness. (1 John 2:5, 5:3, Isaiah 1:19)

2. God's love in me is the well-kept secret within me that this world needs. It is time for me to pour out His love upon others. (Colossians 1:24-27)

3. I am a vessel of God's astounding love in this earth and I share Him with others. (2 Corinthians 4:6, Ephesians 5:8, 1 Thessalonians 3:12, 4:9)

4. God's light is always able to dispel the works of darkness in my life and the lives of people around me. (Colossians 1:13, 1 Peter 2:9)

5. I am commanded to walk in God's love. I daily obey His command. (John 13:34, 14:15, 15:17)

6. I rejoice that I please the Lord because I choose to care only about what He thinks and desires of me. (1 Corinthians 7:23, Galatians 1:10, 1 Thessalonians 4:1)

7. God wants to pour His goodness into me and flow it through me to others. I will allow Him to do it.

8. I daily choose the Father's will in everything, so I will achieve spectacular results. (Luke 9:23-24)

9. Blessings come into my life from God through my obedience to Him. (Deuteronomy 11:27)

My Happy Declarations

1. I have the capacity to give and receive God's great love to seemingly unlovely people.

2. I have Who it takes to love the disappointed souls in this world, because God's love has been poured out into my heart by Holy Spirit. (Romans 5:5)

3. I hope in God, because I know that I will not ever be disappointed. (Romans 5:5)

Joy Keystone

> "What if I speak in the *most elegant* languages of people or in the *exotic* languages of the heavenly messengers, but I live without love? Well then, anything I say is like the clanging of brass or a crashing cymbal. ² What if I have the gift of prophecy, am blessed with knowledge and insight to all the mysteries, or what if my faith is strong enough to scoop a mountain *from its bedrock*, yet I live without love? If so, I am nothing. ³ I could give all that I have to feed the poor, I could surrender my body to be burned *as a martyr*, but if I do not live in love, I gain nothing *by my selfless acts*. ⁴ Love is patient; love is kind. Love isn't envious, doesn't boast, *brag, or strut about*. There's no arrogance in love; ⁵ it's never rude, crude, or indecent—it's not self-absorbed. Love isn't easily upset. Love doesn't tally wrongs ⁶ or celebrate injustice; but truth—*yes, truth*—is love's delight! ⁷ Love puts up with anything and everything that comes along; it trusts, hopes, and endures no matter what. ⁸ Love will never become obsolete. Now as for the prophetic gifts, they will not last; unknown languages will become silent, and the gift of knowledge will no longer be needed. ⁹ Gifts of knowledge and prophecy are partial at best, *at least for now,* ¹⁰ but when the perfection *and fullness of God's kingdom* arrive, all the parts will end. ¹¹ When I was a child, I spoke, thought, and reasoned in childlike ways *as we all do*. But when I became a man, I left my childish ways behind. ¹² For now, we can only see a dim and blurry picture of things, as when we stare into polished metal. I realize that everything I know is only part of the big picture. But one day, *when Jesus arrives,* we will see clearly, face-to-face. In that day, I will fully know just as I have been wholly known *by God.* ¹³ But now faith, hope, and love remain; these three *virtues must characterize our lives.* The greatest of these is love."
>
> 1Corinthians 13 - VOICE

Something To Think About…

Try to imagine how unfulfilling it would be to be in relationship with someone who never communicated with you. It's a very frustrating circumstance. Good communication is one of the keys to a flourishing relationship here in the earth. It is also key to one in the spirit realm.

Like air, water, sleep and food are essential for the body, reading the Bible, and praying are essential to your relationship with the Lord Jesus Christ. It keeps the communication flowing and it promotes health, rest and intimacy with the Lord.

One of the truly joyous gifts you have from God is your ability to pray to and fellowship with Him. It's not a one-sided conversation. He loves to talk to you, so think of prayer as an actual dialogue between you and God instead of the time to recite a list of your wants and needs with an "Amen" tacked onto the end.

Each of the ten keys provided are necessary to have an effective happy, fruitful prayer and praise life. It takes joy, faith, gratitude, commitment, fellowship, wisdom, knowledge of His Word, understanding, willingness, obedience, reverence, love and the fear of the Lord to walk in His authority and power. Remind yourself of these keys whenever you are tempted to feel sad or gloomy.

Today I Pray...

Lord, I am so happy that I have Your love and joy in my heart. Thank You for teaching me to recognize the wonder and the power of Your word, and the importance of truly representing You in this earth. You have made me strong and capable to withstand the negative forces that try to bring me down. I am an overcomer; I am more than a conqueror because You live in me.

I can accomplish and overcome every attack from the devil with the weapon of joy which comes from You, Lord Jesus, because You give me the patience and strength to endure. I no longer live according to my feelings and emotions; I live according to Your Word. You are my Lifeline; I am vitally connected to You. Nothing will ever separate me from your love.

You have given me new hope and a greater awareness of my God-ordained ability to make a difference in this earth. You have opened my eyes to new possibilities and new ways of thinking. I now see myself as a vessel of your astounding love.

I am not limited to the restrictions of a world that eliminates You as the Source of all. I see the power of living a peaceful, joyous, abundant life. I readily embrace living Your kind of life, with a prosperous soul, a healthy mind and a strong body. I thank You that through my life, Your Kingdom and will is seen and being done.

I am so grateful to You for all that You do for me. I am thankful that You are still at work to complete the good work that You began in me. You are my satisfaction and delight. I am honored to be a part of Your family.

I rejoice with inexpressible joy and glory in the reality of my life in You. Thank You for my salvation and all of its benefits. There is nobody else like You. I'm so glad I'm Yours!

You are my reason to *Smile, Laugh and Be Happy.* Hallelujah! Thank You Jesus! Amen!

Scriptures: Romans 8:31, 37, Ephesians 6:10-18
1John 4:4, Nehemiah 8:10, Luke 21:19, Romans 8:35
Philippians 4:13, Matthew 6:9-13, Colossians 1:27
1 John 3:2-3, 1 Peter 1:8, Psalm 68:19, 103:2, 116:12
Philippians 2:13 AMPC, 3 John 2

IT'S TIME TO CELEBRATE AND GIVE PRAISE TO THE LORD!

MY HAPPY DANCE & CLAP SONG

Words by Lonzine Lee
Can be sung to the tune of "The Itsy Bitsy Spider"

First I start to clap my hands,
To celebrate the Lord;
Next I sing this little song,
To You, O Lord alone.

Then it's time to happy dance
And shuffle to the beat,
So I dance and clap to celebrate
And praise Your holy Name.

I'm so happy, I must sing
More of this joyous song,
Lord You are my everything
I'll praise You all day long.
I was blind but now I see
The power of Your Word.
So I do more of my happy dance,
By faith for what I've heard.

I clap my hands to celebrate
And praise Your holy Name.
I do my little happy dance
In remembrance of the same.
My praise goes up before Your throne
And down the blessings come,

As I clap and dance and *sing my song*
To You my God alone.

SMILE. LAUGH. BE HAPPY.

The Scripture and The Science

IN THIS LAST CHAPTER WE are going to look at both the scriptures and the scientific studies that show how smiling, laughing, and choosing happiness affects your brain and body.

We mirror God when we smile and laugh. Remember, He laughs when the world gets crazy.

> *"How dare the nations plan a rebellion. Their foolish plots are futile! Look at how the power brokers of the world rise up to hold their summit as the rulers scheme and confer together against Yahweh and his Anointed King, saying: "Let's come together and break away from the Creator. Once and for all let's cast off these controlling chains of God and his Christ!" God-Enthroned merely laughs at them; the Sovereign One mocks their madness!" Psalm 2:1-4 TPT*

> *"But you, Lord, break out laughing at their plans, amused by their arrogance, scoffing at their sinful ways." Psalm 59:8 TPT*

God smiles at us. His pleasure, expressed through laughter is an expression of His happiness.

"The LORD bless you and keep you; The LORD make His face shine upon you, And be gracious to you; The LORD lift up His countenance upon you, And give you peace." ' "So they shall put My name on the children of Israel, and I will bless them." Numbers 6:25-27

The physical and psychological benefits of laughter and smiling are plentiful. Some research shows that people who consciously (or subconsciously) smile more live better and longer lives. This is not an exhaustive list, but I want to share a few of the benefits of smiling, laughing, and choosing to be happy.

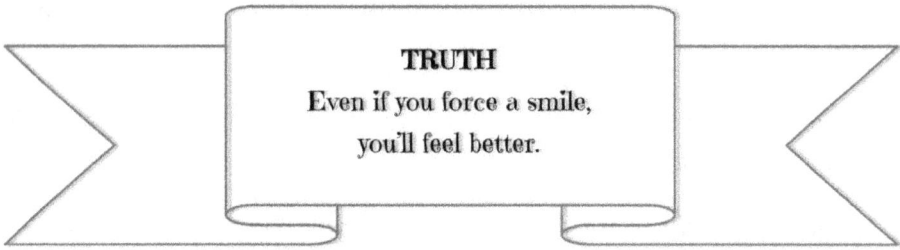

TRUTH
Even if you force a smile, you'll feel better.

While it might not be a genuine Duchenne smile, the kind that involves the muscles around your eyes, you can in fact make yourself feel better simply by smiling.

Your body releases three hormones that make you feel good when you smile. They include dopamine, endorphins and serotonin. These signal to your body that you're happy, and in turn, you feel happier.

◆ ◆ ◆

Author/Entrepreneur Ron Gutman is often quoted for sharing how, *"British researchers found that one smile can generate the same level of brain stimulation as up to 2,000 bars of chocolate."*

Yahoo! Just think, when you smile you can have all of the benefits of chocolate and bypass the sugar high and weight gain. But you, as a son of God, can also experience the pleasure of the Father Himself at the same time.

In the book of Nehemiah the writer declares that the joy of my Lord is our strength. Because He is truly my Lord/Owner, His joy gives me supernatural and physical strength.

This means that I can smile all the way to the doctor's office or the hospital. All the way to the bank, the court, and even the cemetery, if necessary. I can smile because of the supernatural strength I receive through dependency on God.

Neurologically speaking, every time you smile, neurotransmitters activate within your brain. Tiny molecules known as neuropeptides stimulate the neurons in the brain, which then releases the feel-good chemicals endorphins, dopamine, and serotonin.

These are all associated with increasing feelings of happiness, lowering anxiety, and relaxing your mood. Serotonin acts as a natural antidepressant, without the need of the anti-depressant medications used to regulate it. One study even suggests that smiling can help us recover faster from stress and reduce our heart rate.

There's been some evidence that forcing a smile can still bring you a boost in your mood and happiness level. It turns out the benefits of smiling aren't just limited to yourself. It can also affect those around you.

We've already talked about how our brains react when we smile. Doesn't it feel great - isn't it rewarding when you see others around you smile? The reward center of our brain is activated and it makes us feel a little better. Look at countries where the people walk with their heads down. No smiles. It's depressing.

When I walk down the street I'm always smiling. I give somebody a smile because it makes me feel good to see other people and share my smile. And then I laugh a lot, too. Maybe that's why I'm called "The Laughing Doctor" by a number of people.

Plus, I'm really pretty healthy. Don't you think it's better to be affected by smiles, laughter, and people being happy rather than infected by diseases, sadness, depression, oppression, and so on?

In fact, it might be worth your while to practice smiling and see what good things might happen to you. I recommend that you do.

I know that when I choose to smile instead of frown, I have a better relationship with God. I can feel it. Ha ha ha!

Feel-good benefits aside, smiling and happiness can actually affect your job performance. A team of economists performed a workplace study on the performance levels of happy workers. The findings showed that "human happiness has large and positive causal effects on productivity." Positive emotions invigorate human beings, while negative emotions have the opposite effect.

Other studies have found connections with the act of making decisions, how people make process information and learning to the release of dopamine stimulated by happiness, so smiling, laughing and choosing happiness can also make you a more enjoyable, creative and efficient worker. That beats being a bitter, sad, negative or sour person every day of the week.

So the next time you're feeling like you need to be energized, try busting out a toothy or toothless grin that will break into a smile! And if you have no teeth, then gum it!

You will feel so much better. And if you already feel good, smile anyway. You can add joy to someone else's life and help them on their way.

Algorithms and Fractals

The counterfeit version of joy and happiness resonates on a much lower frequency than what God intends for us. Imitation happiness and false joy flow through the soulish nature, operating through emotions and natural, earthly, sensual, devilish sources.

While the joy of the Lord comes from within, counterfeit joy comes through outside sources like sex, alcohol, drugs and other substances, the pursuit of status, riches, material possessions, entertainment, popularity with others, and even **manmade devices or the technology of artificial intelligence**. Let me explain.

While doing this study on algorithms, one thing I found interesting was how deep-learning algorithms were designed to run off an artificial neural network or digital brain. Dictionary.com defines an algorithm as *"a set of rules for solving a problem in a finite number of steps; an ordered set of instructions recursively applied to transform data input into processed data output, as a mathematical solution…or predictive text suggestions."*

So algorithms are used to order a pattern, routine, or procedure written for digital mathematical problem-solving. Computers are instructed to follow a series of repetitive logic loops until they reach a desired or programmed end result or finished work like habits, helpful or destructive.

This article explained how a computer receives the

instruction to process digital stills of fine-art images through a neural network, mimicking the way the neurons in our human brain make connections. The neural algorithm instructs the computer to take the layers of information contained in files and pick them apart piece by piece. It is then able to alter the various layers before putting them back together to create a whole new image. (Lewis, 2016)

What does this mean? Human designed technology uses a manmade device to mimic a God-created function of our brains (artistic expression). God's original creation (humanity) uses human-powered technology to design a program that will artificially recreate an original human brain image. The resultant picture is artificially designed through a false thinking process or pattern. This is an imitation of a divinely artistic original design which mimics the pattern of God's declaration, "Let Us make man in our own image and according to Our likeness." And there are a considerable number of people deriving joy and happiness from the results.

Fractal computer designs (or creations) are another interesting algorithmic development. By feeding the answer of a simple equation calculation thousands of times back to its start, a mathematical fractal is formed. A simple scientific definition of a fractal is "a never-ending pattern that repeats itself at different scales." As the Fractal Foundation states, *"Fractals are SMART: Science, Math, and Art!" "A fractal is a picture that tells the story of the process that created it… Driven by recursion, fractals are images of dynamic systems – the pictures of Chaos."*

Benoit Mandelbrot, a 20th century mathematician is attributed with the concept of fractal dimension. Fractals (derived from French, and the Latin fract which means "broken, or to break") (Stearman, 2009), are complex geometrical patterns that exhibit self-similarity across different scaled sizes. Regardless of the scale you view it in, elements of the overall pattern are infinitely repeated. Think of natural patterns of trees, mountains, coastlines, rivers, seashells, and even galaxies. These are all God-designed.

It is a simple calculation that leads to complexity. These patterns are repeated over and over, looping into a myriad of rotations: hundreds, thousands, or even millions of loops until it reaches the desired result. It follows a pattern to translate the numbers into visual images. The computer's ability to process and repeat the algorithms at increasingly higher speeds is faster than any natural human ability to write, paint, or produce the resulting "reality."

As the computer increases speed, out-processing the natural human brain, the speed set by the algorithm weaves fractions of images that come together in formation of recognizable pictures (fractals) capable of convincing an actual human of their "virtual reality." This is part of the science found in video games, movies, and the like.

We know that the secular world attempts to reverse engineer the creation of God. While it is human brain power that made the discoveries, the direction of excitement went backwards. Honor moved toward what humanity can accomplish instead of toward God and all that He has done. The use of algorithms does not diminish human-brain capacity, which is a choice that people who walk in darkness make.

In the Kingdom of God, what we are capable of producing in the earth surpasses what artificial intelligence can mimic. We operate from the intelligence of The Holy Spirit. As sons of God, our creative Kingdom power is patterned through the WORDS of God that we speak. HIS SPIRIT WORDS create pictures of wholeness, joy, healing, prosperity, etcetera that connect to our brains.

The Mind of Christ within us is the processor that allows the power of God's Word to break through sound barriers and algorithmic limitations of the merely human earthbound mind.

God's WORD moves faster than any computer will ever be able to process information. Even if there is a power outage. God WORD still works.

But as we look at this science, it raises a spiritual question.

Could it be that as we speak the words of life that God has given us, that we also release algorithmic instructions into others? Do we release life into our bodies, into our circumstances with God's Words so that these things that were fractured become whole? Isn't that what Jesus did?

> *Throughout our history God has spoken to our ancestors by His prophets in many different ways. The revelation He gave them was only a fragment at a time, building one truth upon another. But to us living in these last days, God now speaks to us openly in the language of a Son, the appointed Heir of everything, for through Him God created the panorama of all things and all time. The Son is the dazzling radiance of God's splendor, the exact expression of God's true nature—His mirror image! He holds the universe together and expands it by the mighty power of His spoken word. He accomplished for us the complete cleansing of sins, and then took His seat on the highest throne at the right hand of the majestic One.*
>
> *Hebrews 1:1-3 TPT*

What I want you to know is that the vibrations, rhythms, resonance, harmony, and frequency of God in Heaven is quite different from what we operate in here in the earth. As I was sharing this with a group of people, I heard someone ask the question could that be a Divine algorithm? Remember in the beginning the Spirit of God hovered over chaos. God spoke, and when He spoke whatever particles there were in the atmosphere had to come together to form the pictures He saw.

Challenge and Life Work Assignment To Us

Let's create what He has said with our words. Let's do what He does. Let's smile as we sit in the heavens with Him and laugh on the frequency of the Most High. Let's make the true, authentic sound of joy and happiness come through us here in the earth. Because it is finished. It is done. We laugh. We smile, and we walk in happiness because we are living in and from the supernatural world of the finished work.

And those are some of the healthiest and best reasons to *Smile, Laugh, and Be Happy!*

Scriptures: Genesis 1:1-4, 26a, Matthew 8:16, Luke 4:36, 1Corinthians 2:4,13; 4:19-20, 1Thessalonians 1:5, John 3:34, 6:63, Acts 10:44, John 19:30, Matthew 9:22, 15:28-34, Luke 8:48-50, John 5:6; 7:21-24, Acts 4:1-13

Keys to Remember…

1. When I allow Holy Spirit to operate through me like Jesus allowed Him to work in and through Him; then I begin to do the greater works. (John 14:12)

2. Walking by faith is a daily decision. When I choose Him, I choose to walk by faith. (Romans 1:17, 2 Corinthians 5:7)

3. The more of the word of God that I put in me and use, the more I will move forward in my faith. (Acts 17:28, Colossians 3:16-17, James 1:21-25)

4. As my mouth changes to speak His goodness into the atmosphere around me, everything around me changes. Everything is upheld by the word of His power. (Matthew 12:35, Hebrews 11:3)

5. I am training my mind to think like it is a *24/7/365 All-God-All-the-Time Word Network* channel. (Psalm 68:1, 3; John 15:5-10)

6. The Word of God is the only thing I trust. It is the true authority in my life. (Psalm 31:1, 56:4, 71:1, 141:8,119, Proverbs 3:5-10)

7. God will show me how to put it all together. (Psalm 32:8, Jeremiah 29:11-12)

8. I have a lot of good reasons to *Smile, Laugh and Be Happy*! (Psalm 35:27, Isaiah 55:8-12)

FINAL WORDS

Thank you for taking the time to read this little Happy Book. You now have the keys that you need to recognize what has been defeating you. You know how to overcome every obstacle merrily and joyously. The only sad or sorry thing would be if I did not let you know about the One who inspired me in the writing of it.

He is the Deliverer, Healer and Restorer for your life. He makes all things new, wipes out your past mistakes, failures, and sins by casting them as far as the East is from the West. He is the One that gives you a bright, healthy, brand new start.

I'm talking about Jesus Christ, Yeshua HaMashiach – the Messiah. If you do not know Him, I would like to personally introduce you to Him.

This is the most important part of this book. All you need to do is admit that you need Someone greater than yourself to take lordship of your life. Then you simply believe and do what the scripture says. The Amplified Classic Bible says in Romans 10:9-13:

> *Because if you acknowledge and confess with your lips that Jesus is Lord and in your heart believe (adhere to, trust in, and rely on the truth) that God raised Him from the dead, you will be saved. For with the heart a person believes (adheres to, trusts in, and relies on Christ) and so is justified (declared righteous, acceptable to God), and with the mouth he confesses (declares openly and speaks out freely his faith) and confirms [his] salvation.*

The Scripture says, No man who believes in Him [who adheres to, relies on, and trusts in Him] will [ever] be put to shame or be disappointed. [No one] for there is no distinction between Jew and Greek. The same Lord is Lord over all [of us] and He generously bestows His riches upon all who call upon Him [in faith]. For everyone who calls upon the name of the Lord [invoking Him as Lord] will be saved.

Here's a prayer similar to what I prayed when I became born from above. I meant what I said. Lord means Owner, and when I spoke these words, I acknowledged that He owned my life.

"Lord, I need you to be my Savior and Deliverer. Jesus, I believe You died for my sins and that God raised you from the dead. Come into my life and take over. I surrender my life to You. I will obey you. I thank You for my new life. I now belong to and will spend eternity with You. Amen."

I want you to let me know if you pray this prayer or something like it. Call our ministry or email me (the information is at the end of the book). Welcome into the family of Christ!

While this book in no way replaces your Bible, which is the absolute authority and source of God's truth [it is the original Happy Book], consider using this as your, "Run-to-what-God-says-about-being-happy" book. Use it to point you back to His Word and His principles.

God is no respecter of persons, but He truly respects His principles. Put the happy keys into effect, and keep the door open between the Father, Lord Jesus, Holy Spirit and you.

You now know that every bad feeling you have experienced inside is a hangover from your last pity party. Stop accepting the invitations; it is so much more fun to be filled to overflowing with joy, laughter and song.

Congratulations!!! You have made a choice to give up thinking and feeling bad, sad or mad, because you know the truth from the Amplified Classic Bible translation of Proverbs 17:22a:

> "*A happy heart is good medicine and a cheerful mind works healing…*"

Yahoo! And for that truth, you can definitely *Smile, Laugh, and Be Happy*!

BIBLIOGRAPHY
Algorithms and Fractals

https://www.dictionary.com/browse/algorithm

https://fractalfoundation.org/resources/what-are-fractals/

Lewis, D, (2016, May 20). *Smithsonian Magazine.* Retrieved from smithsonianmag.com: https://www.smithsonianmag.com/smart-news/computer-algorithm-can-transform-movies-breathtaking-works-art-180959165/

Stearman, G. (2009, January 5). *BibleProphecyBlog.com* Retrieved from https://www.bibleprophecyblog.com/2009/01/fractals-intelligence-of-gods-design-is.html

Smile. Laugh. Be Happy.
The Culture of God's Kingdom *is*
The King's Will For You

Did you ever stop to think that a laughter-filled life is the King's will for you? Imagine living every day in manifested joy and happiness, exercising supernatural authority over sadness, worry, anxiety, and even oppression as you experience one Holy Spirit-led victory after another. Well, that's the culture of God's Kingdom.

A merry heart does your body good and releases supernatural power to live a powerful, joy-filled life from within. It also changes the atmosphere of the people around you.

This book is about the victorious freedom that The Lord Jesus has provided for you. It is filled with Kingdom keys, exhortations, scriptural insights, a few happy songs with familiar melodies, and a number of "happy facts" and "happy declarations" that you can easily incorporate into your daily life.

Everything that you need has already been provided for you through Yeshua HaMashiach, Jesus Christ. Because He did it all, you don't have to worry.

Believe it. God wants you to *Smile, Laugh and Be Happy.*

Apostle, Dr. Bacer J. Baker (who happens to be a doctor in psychology) is the founder of More Than Enough Ministries Inc., and the apostolic headship over Astounding Love! A Global Church Fellowship & Training Center in Manteca, California. A power-filled ministry gift, author, therapist, serial entrepreneur, mentor, talk show host, and coach, she incorporates the gifting of the Holy Spirit into all that she says and does. As an obedient servant of God, Apostle Baker is a mentor and coach to ministry leaders and entrepreneurs through her coaching business, Biblical Solutions for Life. Apostle Baker enjoys the game of golf as well as spending time with God, family, and friends. She resides in Northern California.

BOOKS BY THIS AUTHOR

The Spirit Of The Fear Of The Lord...In You

And the Spirit of the LORD shall rest upon Him, the Spirit of wisdom and understanding, the Spirit of counsel and might, the Spirit of knowledge and of the fear of the LORD. Isaiah 11:2

How do you see God? Do you think of Him as strict, dictatorial, and judgmental, or does the thought of the Heavenly Father fill your heart with a sense of wonder, joy, awe, and love?

The need to restore honor and reverence of God is paramount in the 21st century Body of Christ. This book takes you on a God-appointed journey to discover what He really means when He instructs us to fear Him.

The righteousness, peace, and joy of His Kingdom will flow from the hearts of those who choose to earnestly live in the identity of sonship. Get ready to discover the power of the Spirit of The Fear of The Lord…In You.

Do You Still Have The CD Version of Your Original Book?

For information on how to order the limited edition original audiobook CD (which contains the audio version of the original *Smile, Laugh, & Be Happy* read by Apostle Baker, Lonzine Lee, and Arayna Sullivan as well as the Happy Songs sing-along) please contact us at:

The Laughing Doctor
P.O. Box 4400
Manteca, CA 95337

Or visit us online at:
www.dominionunlimited.org

Did you pray the salvation prayer? Please contact Dr. Baker directly at tellit2docb@comcast.net

Or call the ministry at 408/945-4439.

www.ingramcontent.com/pod-product-compliance
Lightning Source LLC
Chambersburg PA
CBHW062222080426
42734CB00010B/1996